Strange Gods Before Me

Strange Gods Before Me

MOTHER MARY FRANCIS, *Poor Clare Nun*

*"I am the Lord thy God . . . thou shalt
not have strange gods before Me."*
—*Exodus XX, 2, 3.*

"Walk not after strange gods to your own hurt."
—*Jeremias VII, 6.*

FRANCISCAN HERALD PRESS
1434 WEST 51st STREET • CHICAGO, 60609

Strange Gods Before Me by Mother Mary Francis, **Poor** Clare Nun, was first published in 1965 by Sheed & Ward. Present edition copyright © 1976, Franciscan Herald Press, 1434 West 51st St., Chicago, Illinois 60609. Reprinted with permission of author and publisher.

Library of Congress Cataloging in Publication Data

Mary Francis, Mother, 1921-
  Strange gods before me.

  Reprint of the ed. published by Sheed and Ward, New York.
    1. Contemplative orders. 2. Poor Clares. I. Title.
BX4230.M3   1976   271'.9'7   76-875
ISBN 0-8199-0599-2

Nihil obstat:
   Very Reverend Francis Tournier, S.T.L.
   Censor Deputatus

Imprimatur:
   ✠ *James P. David*
   Archbishop of Santa Fe

   May 21, 1964

Manufactured in the United States of America

To my community,
with love

Author's Note

That these reflections fell into place with the months of the year was not contrived. It occurred. On the other hand, the fact that the ideas of different chapters overlap considerably was both planned and inevitable. The strange little gods here discussed are very close relatives. There is a strong family resemblance, and even many of their mannerisms are the same.

S.M.F.*

Ascension Day
1964

* Sister Mary Francis. After the completion of this book, the author was elected Abbess. Ed.

Contents

Strange Gods Before Me

1

By Way of Introduction:
Heredity and Environment

"Your Excellency, I most humbly ask of you and of our most blessed Order, the grace of a jubilee, that I may prepare myself more surely for death."

There are those who might not consider these just the jolliest possible words for launching a festivity. They might also think it something less than gay to be handed a staff and told in the realistic words of the Roman-Seraphic Ritual to "take this staff of your old age and walk unwearied in the commands of God." Would not one suppose that after fifty years it is time to sit down, rather than to be given a prop for more trudging? But for us that October morning, they were wonderful words, signalling the triumph of a woman's love.

After fifty years of living with the same people day after day, doing the same things month after month, sealed into the obscurity of the same highly restricted quarters year after year, without ever having embellished her wardrobe, changed her coiffure, looked at television or seen a film, a woman might be expected to have arrived at the full ripening of frustration, disgust, and defeat. The product of such an environment would doubtless be a dour old creature with a bleak life behind her and unwelcome death before her. The woman before us this morning, however, was not dour. The tears in her eyes as the monastery tower bells kept pealing and pealing were very evidently not tears of frustration. She was smiling along with the tears, and with the serenity of a woman who has lived a rich and adventurous life to reach the glorious achievement of fifty years. The bells were ringing in the golden jubilee of our Mother Abbess. It was October.

Who will dispute that October is the month of all months for a jubilee? The whole outdoors are goldenly beautiful. Nature has passed her flowering and is rumorously beautiful with approaching death. Everything is gorgeous with fulfilment and mellow with surrender. And this seemed a particularly prodigal autumn. The cloister grounds were all dark reds and burnished golds as we gathered in the chapter room to form the jubilee procession to the choir, and the bells kept on exclaiming that Mother Abbess had now worn the habit of St. Clare for fifty years, while our Steuben glass flashed red and blue and yellow shafts of light about the room.

Now, one of the last things you might expect to find in a Poor Clare cloister is Steuben glass. And it is true that if we had to buy any, the trumpeting angels on the last day would look down on a cloister in Roswell still bereft of Steuben glass. But when our charming friend, the well-known playwright, Dr. Natalie White, insisted that daughters of beauty-loving St. Francis and St. Clare must have a piece of Steuben glass, we accepted her fragilely lovely gift with the same warm gratitude with which we accept rutabagas from the friends who think of our rather different needs. In the heart of the glass are etched those tender words of the dear and rough old fisherman who was the first pope: "The day star arise in your hearts." The glinting prism rested at the feet of our Blessed Mother on the chapter room altar this day, and its red rays struck at the golden garlands draped along the windows.

Given to us back in 1953 for St. Clare's seventh centenary, those handsome garlands had been subjected under Sister Leo's captaincy to swathing, bundling, and reswathing in miles of black tissue paper by nuns determined to keep them everlastingly golden, somewhat in the manner that Sister Anne packs away the white bridal dresses of postulants, so that the stuffed and padded gowns sit up in the boxes, looking alarmingly like headless brides. Sister Leo and her black tissue paper had succeeded. The garlands were still marvelously golden. And Mother Abbess stood under them, looking very small with the tall staff in her hand, and quite outrageously young to be a jubilarian.

Mother Vicaress gave Mother Abbess the candle, wound around with flowers and trailing our best and longest scraps of satin ribbon, and told her to "receive this light and learn by its sign to follow the examples of light," as though this day marked a festival of dawn rather than of twilight. And away we marched to the choir, Postulant Margarita aged three and a half cloistered months leading the way, the abbess of fifty cloistered years bringing up the rear. We all held candles, for this was indeed a *marche triomphale* of a woman who had fulfilled her destiny so well that her one smiling request was for the grace to prepare more surely for her death. A jubilee procession is a death march in the really glorious sense of the term.

So we sang: "O praise the Lord from the heavens!" calling on the angels, the moon, the sun, and the stars for help in our praising. "Fire, snow, mountains, hills," we invited, "praise

Him!" We had moved down the psalm to the verse: "Youths and maidens, praise the name of the Lord!—old folk with the younger, praise His name!" when young Margarita and her immediate contemporaries swung the procession with its older folk into the choir, Margarita looking so worriedly at her candle as to betoken her having received the customary stern warning from Sister Elizabeth, the mistress, in the earlier hours of this glad morning: "See that you don't spill any candle wax on your skirt now!"

Perhaps this dawn-and-twilight, beginnings-and-endings atmosphere was the more pervasive that jubilee day because this particular October had also been the month of the mass wedding, —a dozen of us given over to the Lord by solemn vows at one profession. Cloistered communities are always relatively very small compared with the active orders. Usually each nun makes her solemn vows alone, though there may occasionally be two or even three together. A dozen brides would be phenomenal. This is the way it happened.

Formerly, all cloistered contemplative nuns made solemn vows, which impose a stricter commitment, if not of the heart at least in effect, than do the simple vows made by other religious. During certain persecutions of religious abroad in recent centuries, notably the Kulturkampf in Germany and upheavals in France and Spain, the popes thought it well to prohibit further making of solemn vows with the very stringent obligations of cloister which, among other things, they impose. Then, too, when the Poor Clares came to the United States, this country was considered mission country, being still under the Propaganda Fide, and its religious withheld from making solemn vows. Thus, cloistered nuns, while altering nothing of their way of life in normal circumstances, were deprived for many years of the ancient privilege peculiar to them, the privilege of the most total commitment a woman can formally make of herself to God: solemn vows of religion.

Pope Pius XII changed all this. Deciding that circumstances which had motivated the restrictions previously imposed no longer prevailed, he not only extended permission to resume solemn vows with their obligation of the strict papal enclosure and the official recitation of the Divine Office in choir, but even went so far as to say that communities unimpeded from making solemn vows, and not doing so, were no longer to be called nuns, but sisters, as are other religious.

One after another, communities in Europe and South America, the Orient and the United States—the world—returned to solemn vows. We had to wait until 1960 to get rid of our impediment, which was the lack of a permanent high enclosure wall all around, opaque metal gates, etc., a structure we had not been able to complete for lack of funds. At last came the day when we had all the accessories, and Archbishop Byrne and Monsignor Charewicz came to examine the house and grounds to pronounce them suitable for observing the major papal enclosure. We could make solemn vows!

It was all an extremely official business, we discovered. Holy Church does not take solemn vows lightly. Along with the recommendation of our archbishop, Rome asked a document from the community bearing each nun's signature with the request to take on the obligations of solemn vows. At last the petition was granted, and Archbishop Byrne promised to make the long trip to Roswell in October not once, but twice. He would come on the first and receive the solemn profession of a dozen of his daughters. He would return on the twenty-second for the jubilee of his daughters' mother, their abbess.

The ceremony of solemn vows for a community that had previously observed only simple perpetual vows can be carried out variously, as the ordinary and the abbess wish. It can be extremely simple, with each nun pronouncing the same formula of profession as before, but this time Holy Church accepting the vows as solemn. Or, the entire ceremony of a virgin's consecration as held for each young nun's profession can be repeated. We were jubilant that Archbishop Byrne chose the latter.

So now the stirring ritual of monastic profession was retraced for a dozen nuns, three of whom had been professed for nearly fifty years, one of whom had been professed for a month and a half. It is a strange and wonderful thing to find yourself one of a group making solemn vows in company with your own abbess. There has never been, and can never again be for us, a day quite like that October 1, 1960. Suddenly we, the old and the young of us, were to be brides all over again. So most of the organ music, the singing, the many details fell to the lot of the novitiate Sisters, to their mingled delight and apprehension.

Sister Joel made her first appearance as choir organist before an archbishop, a bishop, and fifteen priests. Novices who had been repeatedly urged to "sing softly until you are more proficient in the chant" were now encouraged to open all their vocal stops. We practised again the ancient ceremonial of profession, the art of falling without graceless mishap to a full-length prostration before the altar, the rising and moving forward and kneeling again for the triple *"Suscipe me"*—"Take me to Yourself, O Lord"—of the solemn commitment, and all the rest. The novices' teeth chattered. Older hearts beat faster.

The day came, ripe with color and pungent with autumn. The leaves were flinging themselves down off the trees in their brilliant dying. We flung ourselves down before God in the mystic death of solemn monastic profession. And the Holy

Spirit presided. The small excitements and bustle of preparation faded away. Sister Benedicta and Margarita rang the great bells for ten minutes; and when they came happily tottering out of the bell tower, Sister Joel began the majestic bridal processional while we stood holding candles, all of us fragrant with the flower corsages Mother Abbess had provided for us. (Who ever heard of a bride without flowers?) Sister Joel played the triumphal *"Ecce, Sacerdos Magnus!"* for our archbishop as though she were accustomed to playing it twice each day while blindfolded. She played the tender *"Prudentes Virgines"* for the brides without a flaw. And the novices sang like birds in spring.

Sister Joel did not much surprise us with her achievement. She has always been a determined sort of person. As fifteen-year-old Priscilla, she read a magazine article about us written by Sister Anne's aunt, and decided this was the life for her. The prospect of going barefoot for the rest of her life particularly enthralled her. So, she wrote to apply for entrance. Reverend Mother informed her that we do not receive girls of fifteen and that Priscilla should pray for guidance and consider the life more deeply (there being considerably more involved in it than going barefoot) until she was eighteen. No reply to this was forthcoming from a Priscilla probably disillusioned to learn that the Poor Clares received only old women of eighteen. Or so we thought. But exactly three years later came Priscilla's second letter, informing Mother Abbess: "I am eighteen now," and asking: "When may I enter?" And after further and rather more detailed negotiations, Priscilla did indeed enter. Suddenly thrust into the position of choir organist for our most solemn ceremony, Sister Joel, now an ancient past twenty, preserved equal calm.

Usually a nun is very young at her profession. She is awed

by the mystery opening before her. It is a different kind of awe which fills the heart when one has lived the monastic life for many years and then receives the privilege of beginning it again with a new dimension.

As we lay prostrate on the bare floor of the choir which still smelled faintly of the epochal waxing Sister Paschal had given it earlier in the week, foreheads on our crossed hands, lips pressing against the boards, flower corsages smelling more sweetly as they were crushed, and while the voices of Archbishop Byrne, Bishop Alfred Mendez, and assorted friars called on the whole heavenly company to pray for us, we could see the universality of the contemplative vocation with new and overwhelming perspectives. Our posture during that litany of all the saints was symbolic of our lives. For this is the real business of the contemplative, to fling herself down before God as a holocaust to Him for the world.

A number of strange little gods have established themselves on high pedestals in our generation. There is the convex god who pushes the world away, a top-heavy god who demands worship of tragic proportions, a surface god who will not tolerate his clients looking into the deeps of life, a neurotic god whose converts are legion in our day, and a few others. It is quite possible for worshippers of the true God to fall under the spell of these idols. Their doctrines are glossy. They have the new look. And they create an environment. In fact, this is their peculiar office.

That October morning, while novices only lately out of high school or college sang their young hearts out for the rest of us, and two bishops and fifteen priests flocked about the altar of the true God to witness the solemn commitment of our womanhood to Him, we really believed there was a second thud when we fell prostrate before the Lord. The first soft thud was that of a dozen nuns dropping to knees and then to faces with a small jangling of rosaries and a concerted swish of long skirts. The second thud could have been that of several strange little gods toppling down in defeat. They just do not thrive in this kind of environment, unless the dwellers work overtime to develop their cults. Daughters of St. Francis and St. Clare are particularly unfitted by heredity to worship them.

All this had gone before the golden jubilee: the marvelous fresh insight into what contemplatives are meant to do and should do for the world and the strong new determination to do it a little more thoroughly. Now, on Mother's jubilee, we had this new dimension of joy with which to fête her. So we made her fabulous gifts like a cake whose top layer, apparently suspended in air, hovered over the underlayers. The cook had evidently had an inspiration from on high. And the cake had icing, because the monastic customs book clearly and happily states that on a nun's jubilee day it is permitted to put icing on the cake. Fifty years, it seems, qualify you for homemade icing, and doubtless condition you to appreciate it, too.

Mother's refectory mug was replaced for the day with our trophy: the gold-banded cup and saucer we had lately acquired from the Quaker Oats Company, Inc. And in the evening we sang the "Compline for a Mother" written by the Latin class, we danced a ballet on the *"Salve, Regina"* under our Lady's picture. And Mother sat, queenly and benign, on her gorgeous throne, an armchair borrowed from the extern Sisters' parlor and covered with a silk parachute. Whoever thinks Poor Clares would have a very restricted use for parachutes is unacquainted with Poor Clares.

What lay at the heart of this golden jubilee, what had earlier cast the jubilarian's daughters down on their faces before the altar of God, is love. The heritage of the children of Francis and Clare of Assisi is love. Our problem is how to exercise it, dilate it, pour it out in the seraphic proportions they did. Cloister environment is that revealing and demanding starkness of extremely simple living. There are no ready-made foxholes against reality in the enclosure. It is always possible, of course, to dig some in your own interior; but, at least, you will have to do the digging yourself and you may be brought up short in your exertions to consider what it is you are doing. The environment problem is really how to make the beautiful most of the reality that confronts you at every moment, unpainted by glamor, of itself impervious to spurious logic, exacting the last farthing from your intellect, your heart, your will.

If St. Francis was too much the realist for the taste of many persons who talked bravely of the realities of life in the thirteenth century and whose descendants are still talking of them in the twentieth, St. Clare was not less so. She meant her nuns to be true women, that is, women fulfilling their destiny by exercising their powers of loving and suffering, and with increasing completeness. Completeness is, of course, a relative term, after all. For capacity for love increases with loving. And so, in the first chapter of her brief rule, she limits herself to two paragraphs.

Paragraph #1 declares that they are to observe the Gospel of our Lord Jesus Christ. Paragraph #2 insists on obedience, to the Church, the pope, the bishop, the successor of St. Francis, and to herself and her successors. It is so typical of Clare. Nothing must be cramped or rigid. Plunged into the Gospel, they were to be inundated with the love and sweetness of the meek and humble Christ. Regulations would spring up naturally enough from this. Yet, she knew that to live by the Gospel according to one's own interpretation without any guidance or restriction of obedience was to open the doors of the Order to heresies unlimited, extremism, and the not remote possibility of the nuns becoming a species of dedicated hobo.

No, they were to live by love, obeying her "more through love than through fear," loving one another, loving every creature under heaven so as to help every creature get into heaven. But they were to do this in the way she would explain in the next eleven chapters! Great spiritual freedom pervades her rule. Great love is her point of departure and arrival. But hard reality upholds both.

To think deeply on the mysteries of life, and to leave off watching the ripples on its surface in order to plunge into the deeps, is to be the only real kind of realist. And it is to this that everything in a contemplative life, whether lived in the cloister under the rule of St. Clare or in those unexpected enclosures in crowds and activity where contemplatives continue to be found outside cloisters, must be orientated. But, what is the meaning of that facile and popular phrase: "to face reality"? God is the great and only Reality off whom our small beings are struck and without whom they would instantly fall back into the nothingness from which His being summoned us. God is.

The farther we depart from the simple concept that God is—and that because, and only because, He is, we are—the less we activate our understanding that "in Him we live and move and have our being" and that our single purpose in life is to know Him and love Him and serve Him. The more we fail to keep before us our glorious destiny to be united with Him forever in eternal love, the less are we true realists. This is, of course, a very different realism from what passes for realism in so much of modern drama and literature.

Realism is not a synonym for sordidness. We face the fact

of sin, whether spectacular and sensational or subtle and self-righteous; we acknowledge that it really exists. But we know that its very reality is an unrealistic approach to our destiny. It is not what God intended. He *is*. He is the only fundamental reality. All life derives from the reality of His Being, and without Him there is no life. Let Him cease to uphold us in creation for a split second, and we shall simply cease to be, all our talk of the realities of life "puffed and burst, as sun starts on a stream." And so, since sordidness and profligacy are never struck off the Being of God, there is a sense in which we can say that sin is unrealistic.

Sin is entirely the invention of man and the fallen angels for which we and they can claim the full inglorious credit. Yet, even for this one entirely personal accomplishment, we had to depend on the Being of God. Ugliness and perversion are unreal in the sense that they merely demonstrate what messes small creatures can make with great and noble powers. They are our negative use of the things of God, just as love is our positive use of them. And the purer love is, the more real it is, the closer to the love of God.

The man and woman faithful in marital love until death despite the increasing small disenchantments of the years are the really sturdy realists, and with a realism much more demanding than the infidelity that sloshes its way through books and drama and life. The young girl who thinks that to dedicate her life on earth to the contemplation which will be the eternal occupation common to all the saved is a very sensible thing to do; who thinks it is, in fact, the most practical of all possible pursuits, and who does it, is a genuine realist. And a nun who has spent fifty years fasting, keeping midnight vigils before the Tabernacle, holding the hurts of the world to the heart of her prayers and trying to sanctify the world's joys with thanksgiving to God, and who is serene and smiling at the end of those fifty years, is a realist of such formidable proportions that when she takes her jubilee staff in hand and her daughters rise up in love around her, the sex-soggy dramatists and the perversion-ridden novelists should bow their heads and slink away.

Goodness and beauty are usually not as easily marketable as evil and ugliness. And there are reasons other than the unfortunate psychological ones for this. Very pragmatic reasons, like the superior talent required to write convincingly and with taste of the enduring reality of good. Virtue is not of itself flashy. Its dramatic or literary expression, therefore, requires a greater craftsmanship.

All this is not in the least to belittle art in favor of piety when we are talking about art. Nor is it even to reopen the tired old debate about whether it is more agreeable to say nothing brilliantly or to say something inanely. God's gifts in a creature always merit and even demand our respect, however the creature misuses them. Two artists who dash off a perfect circle are equally to be commended for the circle, regardless of whether the first artist drew his circle as a representation of the absolute Being of God, and the second as a symbol of nihilism, frustration, and final despair.

A pedestrian poem cannot be praised because the poet attends daily Mass, any more than a play can be denounced as ineffective writing because it flouts moral standards. Saints have no more claim to be indexed in anthologies of poetry than sinners. However, when we have granted all this, there remains the thing that cannot be granted: that the proper field of realism is evil. No, its proper field is good. For evil is, after all, nothing but a negation of good, as sin is a misuse of freedom and perversion supreme misuse of power.

These things are perhaps a little more readily evident in a cloister, where the difficulties of camouflage reach hazardous proportions. There is simply nothing glamorous about praying and doing penance all one's life for a worldful of persons outside one's wall. You have to be quite a tough realist to do this. The contemplative religious woman is never going to be applauded for her lectures or admired for her pedagogy. She has not the satisfaction of exhausting her energies on patients she can see, nor has she much prospect of meeting a martyr's death. Hers is a life of complete, very realistic faith. It must be, or she will not be smiling when she takes her jubilee staff in hand at the end of fifty years of it.

The real and secret glory of the cloistered nun is that she is most often blamed by the world for having given her womanhood as a holocaust to God on behalf of the world. Without pretension, but in all simplicity, she can recall that the world's Redeemer was hated for coming to save the world. Her vocation is to be the complete realist. She takes God on His word that she has chosen the better part; and so she goes on fasting, keeping night vigils, praying, loving, and suffering in her unspectacular way. Her reward is joy. Right realism always begets joy even when, even particularly when, it is most full of suffering.

So, there is nothing unrealistic even in the first approach to the cloistered life. Speaking of prospective postulants, St. Colette says in her constitutions: "We decree that all who desire to enter this Order and who will be admitted, shall have explained to them before they change their attire and embrace the religious life, the austere and difficult things that lead to God and which they shall necessarily be bound to observe steadfastly in this Order, lest at any future time they should plead ignorance." St. Clare and St. Colette want aspirants to this way of life to understand that they are not coming to the cloister to make daisy chains. St. Clare promises them happiness, but only at the price of self-oblation, the happiness increasing as the holocaust becomes more total.

Now, I am somewhat hampered in writing this, being at the moment reduced to scribbling across only half the page and with one hand impeded. The reason is reddish-gold and white. It is a three-weeks-old kitten sitting on the other half of the page, its little white forepaws resting on my left hand and its small sandpapery tongue licking my fingers. But these are the realities of literary composition one must face in the cloister, just as one must face certain bizarre realities in the menu.

There is, for instance, a peculiar Poor Clare entrée called "prune soup." And it is called prune soup because this is exactly what it is: buttermilk prune soup. After a certain period of time, depending on one's personal powers of adjustment, one gets first accustomed to, and then quietly devoted to, this strange concoction, which we are assured, and which we believe in all good faith, is very nourishing. Whether it has been handed down directly from the holy founders or is an interpolation by one of their more imaginative spiritual descendants can no longer be determined from the mass of truth and apocrypha about the Order. But it does appear to be a brew reserved to the Poor Clares without challenge.

Once a Sister from Canada was visiting our extern Sisters for several weeks. She lived in the extern part of the monastery and shared with them the cloister fare which is given out on days the Sisters do not prepare their dinner separately. The day arrived for prune soup. Sister Monique, who had come from a section of Canada which was strictly French-speaking and whose English was a little uncertain, smiled with amused tolerance on beholding and stirring the soup, and alerted our extern Sisters: "Someone has drop ze prune in ze soup."

When this was relayed to us at recreation, Sister Margaret remarked: "Well, it was a very charitable way to look at it. She didn't want to think anybody had put prunes in the soup on purpose." And she added meditatively: "After all, what would you have thought at home if you had found a banana in the consommé?"

But we know the prunes are meant to be there, and we accept rather than explain them. In fact, I have known novices who were such thorough-going realists that they suspected the validity of any departure from these refectory-realities.

On prune soup days, Mother Abbess announces from the head table, and not, I fancied when I was a postulant, without a touch of grimness: "Dear Sisters, there are three prunes for each Sister." One day she did not make the customary announcement, for we had no prunes. The soup was a stark affair: prune soup without prunes. It was my week to serve in the refectory, and I shall never forget one determined novice plunging the soup ladle down into the deep tureen again and again in a quite literally fruitless effort to bring it up laden with prunes. Each time, she would stare incredulously at the pruneless ladle. Finally, mercy compelled me to lean over and whisper: "There are no prunes in the prune soup today." Nor shall I ever forget her expression on hearing this. Shock. Unbelief. Alarm. For this realist knew that life is meant to be beset with trials and that heaven comes only afterward. She was learning in the novitiate that the cloistered life of hard faith cannot be lived sentimentally, romantically, or euphemistically. Where there is prune soup, one should face the prunes.

2

The Surface God

One cannot cut through appearances to their inner significance without using the vision of faith. And the eyes of faith see at first painfully, straining after shapes, peering into actions with a kind of enchanted bewilderment, rather like the blind man of the Gospel whose sight was restored to him by the Master, but who first saw men walking like trees and only later on saw men walking like men. The Scriptures delicately veil his secret as to when he began to see men walking as images of God and to penetrate something of the mystery each man is given to reveal to all other men. His new vision kept growing clearer, sharper, nearer to the absolute. The eyes of faith do the same.

When surface vision is put by, and the vision of faith substituted, the enchanted bewilderment of our former blind man of the Gospel is experienced on a loftier plane. It never quite disappears, as the eyes of faith grow clearer. But it is the bewilderment which steadily diminishes, and the sense of enchantment which marvelously grows.

It is, after all, better to see men walking like trees than to see self-propelled bipeds describing meaningless circles. The concept of a walking tree opens wide and completely delightful avenues of expectation. A tree has reached a new level of existence. We are transported to the outer space of thought, trying to fathom the mystery. The man in the Gospel, squinting at the supposed walking trees, was probably thinking with much more penetration than some of his contemporaries who did not consider the busily trotting rational creatures around them much worth watching, and consequently never saw them at all.

Surface vision is the reduction of adventure to routine, and a great blaze to the dimensions of a gas-jet. People with surface vision deal with immediate significance rather than with ultimate meaning. And so they imperil truth. But if surface vision is everywhere perilous to truth, it is nowhere more so than in religious life. And in the cloister it is fatal.

In the recent rash of books and pamphlets on the cloistered life, writing which covers the field from girls leaping in over footlights and out over walls, to the less sensational ones who walked firmly in on high heels, and then walked the cloister round on bare feet until the day when their companions slid them into the cloister burial vault, surface vision is often all too clearly present. The curious thing about it is that it takes two very different forms.

In the worst of the books and pamphlets, literarily speaking, a cozy religiosity pervades all. Brave and smiling nuns are daily wound up by the abbess, key of custom held firmly in hand, and run like good little trains around the customary track. They do not have to think. The rule thinks for them. They have no problems, for obedience solves all problems. They fast determinedly, and feast on the satisfaction of having fasted. They rise at night, and repose securely on the fact of having done penance. They have put their free wills, judgments, opinions, and ideas in the monastery locker. It is the simple life. And it is true, at least, that such a life should appeal to simpletons.

On the other hand, in the best of these books and pamphlets, also literarily speaking only, cloistered nuns are women whose lower lips are bitten through, nails chewed down to the quick, and psyches ridden with neuroses because they are daily forced into a routine of traditional observance, have their personalities stretched out of shape on the rack of regulations, and their talents crushed by monastic custom. The reader is given appalling glimpses of What Goes On. He is shown intelligent women, many of whom have been exposed to higher education, made to do thoroughly ridiculous things like bowing low when they meet the abbess, folding their table napkins always into three precise creases, wearing a long, hot habit when it is cold, and a long, hot habit when it is hot, marching precisely in procession, taking the same place in the refectory every day. And when the reader is properly conditioned by these confidences, the exposé is made: they sometimes even kneel before the abbess, as though she were a goddess!

(Where is the fearless writer who will urge that the army abandon uniforms, that ensigns sit in the admiral's place in mess if they feel the urge, that soldiers stop saluting officers, and that in army drills a man march in time or out of time according to the promptings of his personality drive?)

A man can be a good soldier without shining his shoes. He can be of heroic stuff without squaring the corners when making his bed, or without making the bed at all, for that matter. But now everyone will exclaim: How ridiculous! For everyone thrills to disciplined troops, men whose personalities are too powerful to need expression in wearing shorter trousers or longer haircuts than the rest, whose characters are too virile to require breaking through regulations to make their impact on the world.

If we put surface vision by, we shall come to cry: How preposterous! to a number of current hypotheses on the spiritual life. Saints see into the deeps of earthly existence, which is the immediate reason why they are fitted to receive from God insight into eternal life. Saints never spend their lives standing on the shore of life. They "strike out into the deeps and let down their nets." And they always bring up a catch. Neither do saints dwell on the edge of their own souls. They cast themselves into the depths and discover who they are, why they are living, and what the whole business is about.

This is certainly patent in St. Francis and St. Clare of Assisi. They held the key to life's mysteries because they did not just see things or people. They saw *into* things and people. To Francis and Clare, creation was a vast symbol, and they spent their lives deepening and sharpening their power of interpreting it. Everything was fraught with mystery, touched with symbolism, tingling with wonder. This is one of their sublimest heritages to their children. To live in a cloister and see only things as things and people as people is never to crack the shell of mystery which encloses the true contemplative community life.

One could select any day out of many monastic days, any incident, even, to demonstrate this. The great November Straw Saga will do.

Sister Benedicta had the red-and-black stocking cap pulled well down over her veiled head when she came outdoors this November day. The leather jacket someone's brother used to wear for skating was zippered over her habit. She walked determinedly toward the novitiate porch, piled end to end and three feet high with straw, wriggling her bare toes as her out-door wooden sandals slapped at the driveway. November can be cold in New Mexico, but straw mattresses have to be made despite the weather. And if the monastery quarters do not allow of setting up a straw mattress factory inside, the obvious solution is to set it up outside.

So the novices in their leather jackets, woolen scarves over their white veils, sat in the circle of thin November sunshine, perched on their apple-box benches, and waited for Sister Benedicta's return.

Now, the novitiate porch is a perfectly lovely porch and has every practical advantage for those desiring to enter it from within the novitiate. That is to say, it has a door. For those aspiring to get on the porch from the yard, however, it presents certain problems. Its railing is perched more than five feet above terra firma, and it has no steps. This inaccessibility is due to no interesting architectural quirk in the abbatial mind which planned that wing of the monastery, for actually a stairlessly aloof novitiate porch offers no major, much less insoluble, problem. Novices in cloisters are expected to be philosophers. And a philosopher knows there is only a restricted need for stairs when one has legs. Sister Benedicta's advantage is that her Creator endowed her with very long ones. There are handy clefts in the brick sides of the porch. One has only to plant one sturdy wooden sandal in the lower cleft, the other foot in the higher cleft, swing leg #1 up over the rail, follow with leg #2, and,—one has arrived. It is possible, of course, to go through the novitiate hall and out the side door upon exit, as also to go in the side door, down the novitiate hall, and out through the novitiate for porch entrance. But this is all very tame, unimaginative, and time-consuming when one can easily climb the porch. Sister Benedicta accomplished this feat with her usual skill and recollection, pulled the red-and-black stocking cap a little more firmly over her ears, and surveyed the situation.

The situation involved piles and piles of straw, some mouldy, some mouldier, and some in a blessed state of preservation from mould. The task was to extricate these latter and fling them over the porch rail to a novice-aide who would rush the load to the rest of the crew on their apple boxes. Sister Benedicta jumped up on the piles of straw, kicked some disapprovingly, fingered others, and finally applied the International Sniff Test. The straw that survived these gruelling examinations was then tossed down to Sister Maria, who flung it into a coffin-sized box and dragged it over to the waiting experts. One does need to be expert to sort straw.

By this time it was three o'clock, and Sister Dolores began the customary prayer: "O Jesus, God of love and mercy, I am sorry I have so often passed this hour without recalling the love which urged Thee to die for me a most cruel death upon the Cross." Hands swooped down on the new supply of straw and began the sorting and assembling process.

The Roswell menagerie had considered the truckload of straw brought in by obliging Texan farmers about the best thing that has happened in the cloister since they set out on their appointed life's task of getting the upper hand with the nuns. Rubra, the cat, promptly built herself a straw shelter and brought forth red-and-gold quintuplets. Lulu, the cow, thought the whole thing was arranged entirely for her comfort and nutrition, and mooed with becoming gratitude. The more precocious of the kittens had reached the age for forty-yard dashes before the end of the Great Straw Saga. This day, they had quite got the spirit of the thing, jumping down from one novice's lap to rub against another novice's ankles, and following the tossing of the straw with the ecstatic mews which are a very young kitten's substitute for meows.

Sister Benedicta stood back on the porch, gauged once more the familiar distance to the ground, pulled again at the stocking cap, and jumped. She landed with the aplomb Roswell novices develop from frequent porch-leaping, and walked sedately over to join the group. After all, she is the senior novice. One has one's dignity and responsibility. Memory flashed back the picture of Sister Benedicta's entrance into the monastery from the girls' college where she had been majoring in art, spotlighting the extremities: the peg heels and the shaggy haircut. (Incidentally, cloistered nuns keep abreast of current styles and coiffures by the brief glance they get at a new postulant clicking her way into the choir to receive the cape and veil. After several sobering experiences with the hair styles of incoming postulants, one old nun remarked with satisfaction at the recreation after the entrance of a new postulant: "Isn't it lovely!—they are wearing hair again!")

The kittens mewed and leaped. Lulu gave some baritone moos rather surprising in a cow of so distinctly feminine a personality. And Sister Dolores' voice travelled down the phrases of the ancient monastic three o'clock prayer: "By His wounds, His death, His precious blood outpoured for all mankind, pardon all our sins." It was evident from the pursing of Sister Gabriel's lips that she was tuning up to hum: "O come, O come, Emmanuel!" as soon as the prayer was done. For Sister Gabriel usually hums discreetly at work, unless of course she is in a place apart where she can abandon humming for singing. Sister Maria gave the finished straw some professional pats into place. Well over a year has passed since her long journey with her parents from a far-distant state to

Roswell. "I'll be there as soon as I take the semester exams," the college freshman had written breathlessly. She has shown equal despatch in the business of monastic living.

Now, there are two ways to view this November scene. One way is to see some peculiarly garbed young girls engaged in the drab task of sorting straw. Another is to see some fledgling contemplative nuns occupied with the important business of making straw mattresses which have been the beds of Poor Clares since St. Clare started a new way of life for women back in 1212. Whether one thinks a stocking cap over a veil is preposterous, sorting straw a task for morons, and inaccessible porches only what one would expect to find in a place like this; or whether one finds something moving and quite possibly poetic in the vision of frail November sunlight slanting over young novices pink-cheeked in the cold and laughing at the antics of young kittens, whether one senses that there is a deep mystery hidden beneath the surface of appearances here, depends on the kind of vision one has: of the surface or of the deeps.

We can cry: Waste! waste! at intelligent young girls sorting straw. But we had better first find out what it is that intelligent young girls sorting neuroses and boredoms are saving.

Boredom seems to be the inexhaustible theme of many modern novels. At least, this is the impression the cloister librarian gets from the current book reviews, since we do not indulge in novel-reading. What do people get bored with? The banal, the pointless, the meandering path that leads nowhere. This is why, although there have always been and will always be suffering contemplatives and weary contemplatives as the cycles of the spiritual life keep turning, there will never in this real sense be a bored contemplative. However obscure the goal, and even the point of it all, may seem at the times when faith is tried by God, there is still a very objective goal. There is definitely a point. And the cloister path does not meander. In fact, that is precisely why it is a difficult path; it leads so straitly to our destination.

Thinking is a very demanding process at times. Jargon, clichés, and the shibboleths of the moment provide padding for the brain under a protective coat of spurious logic. These things must come off if we are to do any real thinking of our own, and especially if the eyes of faith are to function. If they do not function, we shall be reduced to surface vision, seeing things and people, but never meanings. And if it is sometimes painful to think, it is also very invigorating once we get braced to it. As with Francis and Clare of Assisi, things begin to take new shapes before us. Wonderfully, their true shapes.

It may indeed be outrageous to kneel before an abbess because she is a goddess when she is not, but it is very sensible sometimes to kneel before an abbess because she directly represents God. It would be as silly as claimed for one woman to step aside and bow to another woman when the corridor is quite broad enough for two to pass, but it makes a great deal of symbolic sense for a nun who has delivered her life and all its details over to God by a solemn vow of obedience made in the hands of that abbess, to bow to the one who holds her commitment. There is something to be said for nuns preferring to be uncomfortably warm in summer and not cosily warm in winter when we remember the numbers of women who flaunt all Christian modesty in summer and court sensuality in winter.

If some well-intentioned writers insist it is nonsensical for adult religious to ask routine small permissions, one suspects that some adult layfolk would think it time and words well spent to obtain soap and ink, aspirin and toothbrushes, merely by humbly asking for them. Some would call it a very good bargain.

To pretend there is anything at all more important to do than to love and serve God in the way He wishes us to love and serve Him is to live the hollowest of delusions. When young Lady Clare Offreduccio became the first contemplative Franciscan nun, most of her relatives and more of her friends also cried: Waste! living death! burial! But after seven centuries, the name of St. Clare is only a little less famous on earth than in heaven, and young girls are still fired by her ideals to live a life of penance and prayer for the world. One is inclined to wonder how many people would remember Clare in 1965, had she "used her talents" as the neighbors urged. Or even how many would have remembered her in 1265.

One of the most delightful modern ironies is that the charming girl who disappeared out of the thirteenth-century world to pray for the world in a cloister, who buried her talents and wasted her life by all the best worldly standards, has been chosen patron of television in the twentieth century. She meant her daughters to hold the whole world in their spiritual embrace, and now as the boundaries of our world begin pushing into outer space, she surely intends them to widen their embrace accordingly.

But what does all this have to do with sorting straw? A great deal.

A thing is perfect when it achieves the end for which it was made. A life is perfect when it fully accomplishes its purpose. The great purpose of the contemplative life is to wait upon God directly and to give testimony. The office of the beloved is to be at the beck and call of the Lover. The call may be to do or to suffer, to sing or to listen, to labor or to rest in His arms. She never knows what the call of each new day will be. She only waits.

"Tuus sum" is the single cry of the contemplative to God. "I am Yours,—and do please feel quite free to do whatever You wish with me." Not doing something for God, but being someone for God is the most powerful testimony one can give to the pre-eminence and supereminence of God. In a sense it is a greater testimony than physical martyrdom, since this kind of witness is a matter not of an act but of a state. And this kind of dedication, this kind of testimony, is a very great work in the Church.

Dom Columba Marmion has gone on record (in the good company of St. John of the Cross and an imposing number of the saints) as holding that the soul immolated to God in the nudity of pure faith and perfect union does more for the whole Church in an hour than others do in their entire lives. Such immolation is, of course, by no means the restrictive goal of enclosed nuns. Doubtless we shall have some glorious surprises in eternity when the heroic sanctity of the salesclerk, the actress, and the housewife are revealed. However, such immolation is very proper, if not peculiar, to the cloistered nun. It is, in fact, required of her by the nature of her vocation. And so the contemplative nun does not sit back and preen herself on such statements. She bows her head very humbly before them, knowing that she has been called to this intimacy with God in the cloister so that she may do a great work for the Church just by being His, but knowing also that "just to be His" is the most demanding of elections toward which she must bend all her energies and in which nothing of hers may be reserved for herself.

Hans Urs von Balthasar writes with profundity of that self-abandonment which gives such glory to God and which figures so prominently in His plan of salvation as being the particular office of the contemplative. It is at once the suffering of the contemplative life, demanding as it does a real fierceness of faith in God and His word, and also the glorious adventure-someness of that life. Each day in the cloister is a new and rare adventure. We wait. What will He ask today? We do not know. So all the resources of one's being must be flung down before God to be used or not used as He wishes.

Anyone with only surface vision can sort straw, after a fashion or with varying efficiency. But only the eyes of faith see in the straw a repose for a tired spouse of the most high God at the end of a day of prayer and penance and toil, as straw once made a bed for the most high God himself. It then becomes very important to sort straw with care, to lay stalk carefully alongside stalk, to pack straw with exactitude into the ticking cover. And it is a particularly dear task to perform in November when we await the anniversary of the birth of the Child of the straw and the manger, to whom St. Clare so tenderly appeals in her rule as Witness supreme of that life of poverty and naked faith which she lived and outlined for her daughters and which, in its turn, bears witness to Him: "the most sweet Child Jesus wrapped in poor little swaddling clothes and laid in a manger." Seen thus with the eyes of faith, sorting straw is obviously a task pointed definitely toward the achievement of an end, and it is not less important than carving the stations of the Cross which Sister Benedicta executed last year or producing the poem Sister Assumpta wrote last month.

All the nuns in a cloister are giving testimony to the greatness of God simply by being nuns in a cloister. Where there is only surface vision, all the strict prohibitions and austerities of the cloister and all its minutely searching demands are as obsolete in this busy modern world as certain modern crusaders insist they are. In fact, they are as foolish as the life itself and just as invalid in an age concerned more with astronauts than with elevation of soul, with physical outer space more than with mystical union with God. With every breath they draw, contemplatives are silently swearing that there is nothing greater or grander, nothing more significant, modern and valid than simply being at God's disposal. This is why cloistered nuns take one another's external achievements so much for granted and are so casual in their joy over one another's accomplishments.

There is now in circulation an imposing tome which proposes to study, to dissect really, a great modern saint who was a contemplative. Character and personality analyses of some members of her community are painstakingly made. The rest are disposed of in one phrase: "The others were unimportant." At our next recreation Sister Beatrice remarked wryly: "Well, I am glad there aren't any unimportant people in our community." The whole thing hinges on what we consider important, the surface or the deeps.

When Sister Assumpta's young nephew was suddenly killed and the impact of the sorrow moved her to write a poem, Mother Abbess read it to us at recreation and we responded with appreciation for a beautiful thing. When this first poem of hers was accepted for publication in one of the most distinguished magazines of poetry in the country, we were all proud of the author. But when we see Sister Assumpta hoeing up weeds on the west drive, no one tsks or tuts that our new poet is doing work beneath her station.

Sister Celine has lately invented a new method of producing linoleum cuts, and her finished products are a delight to behold. But this in no way makes her a person apart. Her drawings are passed around at recreation and heartily admired. And when she won the princely sum of $10.00 in a Lenten recipe contest with her formula for "monastery lentil soup," we congratulated her and laughed with her and begged her to stop painting and concentrate on earning more hard cash for the monastery's shallow coffers. Today Sister Celine has been carrying bricks most of the day, laying a path in the patio. And her bricks give witness to the glory of God as convincingly as do her linoleum cuts.

It is on the surface that things seem important of themselves. In the deeps, they are always seen as only relatively important. And one of the sturdiest manifestations that nuns are living a life of faith and not of appearances is this very simplicity with which external accomplishments are treated. Out of this simplicity flow many of the joys of the cloister, too.

In 1959, one of us wrote a play about St. Teresa of Avila. *La Madre* was produced at Notre Dame University during the summer session and then at Blackfriars Theatre off-Broadway. God blessed it with success and the secular critics were very generous. What did this mean in our community? It meant that the Sisters wrote a script of their own and produced it as a live "TV" show for a recreation surprise. One immortal line was that of the usher at Blackfriars dashing wildly from the theatre to report that "the crowds are simply pouring out from *La Madre*,—and it's only the end of the first act!" The production included shots of the author apprehended on the fire escape at Blackfriars, having fled the cloister to take in her play, and being sternly ordered home to help with the weeding. It ended with the decision to send her to Morocco to work in the banana groves until the African sun had dried up "this ceaseless flow of composition."

What does this nonsense prove? Well, for one thing, it demonstrates love; and for another, quite a nice sense of values. When we live very simply and love very simply, we can tease very outrageously. But more than this, it is evidence of the vision of the deeps. Since nuns are communally given to God, but with the most individual of commitments because it is so absolute, to bear testimony to the world of His supremacy, they have a very different gauge for "importance" from that of the do-ers and the hustlers who are content with surface vision. Thus, they are not too much impressed with external achievements. They merely accept them and casually rejoice in them. And no one wastes time or effort in being coy about such things, knowing that false diffidence about God's gifts is admitting to the heresy of thinking they are one's own gifts. Each one's accomplishments are everyone's joy.

And since each one's is everyone's, there is no need to be acquisitive. We do not all clamor for harp lessons because Sister Gabriel plays the harp. We marvel at Sister Beatrice's fabulous pink pudding on Gaudete Sunday as at a community achievement. All are helped to realize, from the novitiate days, that the really great achievements are interior, just as the great battles are fought in the inner court of the soul and the lasting accomplishments registered only in the heart of God. Thus, inability to rejoice in the gifts or the external achievements of others, while it is an unhappy state of being in any community, is something of a real tragedy in the cloister. One who is determined to "shine," to do notable things instead of a single notable thing, and who is troubled at thinking herself outshone, has done a very odd thing in coming to a cloister at all, and has shown herself highly unrealistic in the choice.

In this same way, all the minutiae of religious life are given the deference they deserve as symbols of a great reality, though of themselves they might appear as exaggerated, cumbersome, or formalistic; maybe as mere nuisances. This is where so many of the errors that beget Impassioned Authors to correct them originate,—on the surface. *"Tuus sum."* I am Yours, God. Not, "I must loosen the collar of this regulation-shirt so that I can really do something for You, God." What mental strutting about we do when we talk of doing something for God! What can we do for Him but love Him? And how can we love Him more profoundly or comprehensively than simply by being His? It is not only the greatest act of doing, this just being; it is also the most demanding and the most adventurous.

When we are forced to come to grips with a crisis, even only a physical crisis, of urgent personal proportions, we not only discover the unreality of certain self-styled realists, but also the meager rewards of surface vision. When our benefactors brought the news of the Cuban crisis of 1962, and Mother Abbess gravely relayed to us the information that we might shortly be annihilated in atomic warfare, we were duly impressed. Extra penances were planned, extra prayers for peace were offered. Yet, at recreation, when Sister Anne suggested that if nuclear destruction did visit us, it would be perfectly lovely, really, to have the community die together, all in one piece so to speak, and arrive in eternity on a single schedule, a very serious discussion followed, led by Sister Assumpta, as to whether it would not be better if a few were spared so that they could build up a future community. And would anybody offer, given the choice, to remain behind; or would everybody favor the one departure? You have to have something deeper than surface vision to sort out one another's deaths and your own so serenely.

It is the same with sorting straw or sorting death. Surface vision turns from the first and considerably more quickly from the second. Vision of the deeps knows that things are important insofar as they are God's Will and done for God's love,

no more, no less. To devote one's whole energy to the most
intimate service of God is not to waste anything. It is, in fact,
to demonstrate a rather unique sense of thrift. For nothing so
immediately insures that nothing of ours will be lost as does
giving ourselves to God without intermediary.

All this is part, only a very little part, of the thinking of the
girls who could have been any number of other things on a
given November afternoon instead of straw-sorters in a cloister in Roswell. The next afternoon they may be printers,
sweepers, painters, organists. It does not matter. But it ex-
plains why they pray while they work and sometimes laugh
while they work. They are simply young girls who have
stopped worshipping the surface god and started looking into
the deeps. Once the surface god is dethroned, the other
strange gods of our generation are not so hard to topple.

3

Continues the Surface God

In our days, everything is open to question. And everybody wants answers. The authority of the hierarchy is being reinvestigated. The position of the layman in the church is being reassessed. The priesthood is being renovated, and the vocation of the religious woman engaged in the active apostolate re-evaluated. Everybody wants to know where everyone else stands, why he is standing there, and whether he really has a right to occupy the space.

With the studies of seminarians being redirected and the whole structure of religious life being closely investigated, what about the cloisters? Pope Pius XII, Pope John, Pope Paul, each has told us in his own idiom that the religious as well as the layman is expected to keep up with the times. Some Council Fathers of Vatican II have made the same point in greater detail and with such considerable vigor as to rattle the beads of many a religious and ruffle the pages of many a convent customs book.

Cardinal Suenens of Belgium has presented a clear and sympathetic case for the adaptation proper to religious women of our century. Again, what about the cloisters? For they, too, are always open to question. They have the answer. But disciples of the surface god will never find it, since it does not appear on the surface; and the surface is all he can see.

Has the day at last arrived when enclosed nuns should be liberated to "do something useful"? Is it time to stop living in silence when there is so much to be said? Are grilles and disciplines, fasts and bare feet, night vigils and solemn choral offices definitely out of style? It is easy for the contemplative nun to bristle at such questions, but it is much better to face them and answer them.

To write off the purely contemplative religious life as superfluous to our times must surely be the dearest desire in the heart of the surface god. For to maintain that a state of being is no longer necessary in the charged atmosphere of doing is to score the triumph of superficiality. Religious dress can become outmoded to the point of being ridiculous. The customs of religious Orders can obviously call for readjustment, not only from century to century but sometimes even from generation to generation. Schedules and horaria can need revising. Even secondary aims may need rethinking. But there are fundamentals in religious life, in all life, which do not and cannot change.

You may change all the pictures on all the walls in a house, repaint it, remodel it, and it will be the same house, only greatly improved. You can also take out the supporting beams, or dig into the foundations; and the house will shortly become a heap. Adaptation is intelligently achieved on accidentals only by those who are quite certain about the nature of accidentals and the nature of fundamentals, and who can distinguish the one from the other.

We can update customs. We cannot update the idea of self-immolation. We do well to rip anachronistic fringes off religious life, but less well to rip its seams. Certain needs arise in the Church in one century and are no longer pressing in the next century. And so religious Congregations founded for a particular need set their sights in another direction. On the other hand, the need for prayer and penance is independent of century or social milieu. That many dedicated souls should labor in the vineyards and a few keep watch on the mountain has been the need and program of the Church through all the centuries. This is not subject to change, since it is God's immutable design that some religious should have Him for their entire occupation. Christ said of Mary sitting at His feet: "It shall not be taken away from her."

The enclosed contemplative life will be outmoded only when love is outmoded. A community pledged to praise God day and night in the choral recitation of the Divine Office, to adore Him unceasingly, to channel His mercies to the world, to help repair by its penances chinks made in the walls of the Church, needs no sideline activity to justify its existence in 1265, 1965, or 4265. In his third radio address to contemplative nuns throughout the world on August 2, 1958, Pope Pius XII declared: "Others live nothing more than the contemplative life, both by law and in fact. They must remain faithful to this, unless they are bound by necessity, and for a limited period of time, to take up certain apostolic activities. It is obvious that these strictly contemplative nuns take part in the apostolate of love of neighbor by the three forms of example, prayer and penance."[1]

However, if a strictly contemplative community does not

[1] Three Radio Addresses of Pope Pius XII *to Contemplative Nuns Throughout the World*, reprinted in *The Pope Speaks*, ed. Michael Chinigo (New York, Pantheon).

need apostolic activities, it does certainly need the religious and the layfolk devoted to a more active form of apostolate, quite as much as the active religious and the laymen need the contemplative community. A heart is meant to keep pumping blood to the members. If there are no members, the heart may as well stop.

That was a terrible thing, that quiet declaration of the Mother of God to the children at Fatima: "Many souls go to hell because there no is one to pray and do penance for them." Cloisters are built, stand, and endure simply because some people do want to pray and do penance for a multitude of people they have never seen but dearly love. And cloisters will go out of style only as God goes out of style.

So much for the fundamental concept. The question of the individual contemplative religious is a different one entirely. She can get very much out of current style, usually because she never discovered any current in the first place. For, though the enclosed life of prayer and penance is a life so profoundly demanding as quite to escape the vision of the surface god, it is equally true that the danger of superficiality is nowhere so great as in the cloister. Precisely because her vocation is to the profoundest self-immolation, the contemplative religious woman can establish her own peculiar form of escapism on the surface of her own life.

There is no shallow water for the contemplative to wade in. She has either to plunge into the deeps or spend her life floating on the surface. And of all superficial forms of womanhood, surely none is so macabre as the superficial contemplative. She is indeed a contradiction in terms. Unfortunately, there can be many supposed justifications, even encouragements, for it in the cloister.

By its nature, the enclosed contemplative life is the freest and most direct path to union with God. Paradoxically, its nature demands a stricter regimen to achieve this end. And in the very minutiae which are intended to liberate her spirit from the chains of worldliness and self-involvement, a nun may commit herself to life imprisonment and almost complete self-absorption. The strict rules, the many regulations, the ancient customs of the monastic life are all meant to be gateways into the open courts of God's love, into that spiritual freedom which is possible only by way of discipline. Minutiae must be seen as things of grace and beauty, not as balls and chains. The pity is that we can develop an unhealthy affection for balls and chains. The type of individual who does this lays a threat against the life she has superficially elected but never understood. And often enough it is the life which is blamed for her mistake.

Undeniably, there are those who prefer not to think if it is at all avoidable. Wherever such persons decide to live, the last place should be in a cloister. A life orientated directly to God, without intermediary, demands of its followers not only profound love but profound thought. Yet there still lurks at enclosure doors the ghost of that false spirituality apparent in many writings and conferences of the past century, the ghost which warns that profound thinking is suspect in a contemplative, and that once a girl steps inside the enclosure any need to exercise her powers of reasoning automatically ceases.

If pursued to its logical end, this idea will be seen as designed to reduce human beings to a lower order of creation. God's sublime gift of intellect to men is not to be either feared or discarded in the cloister. The contemplative life is not for irrational beings. The mystery of the purely contemplative vocation is so deep that after twenty years of experiment in it, a nun may very properly feel that she is just beginning to penetrate its meaning.

It is difficult to understand where the thesis of the unthinking nun was formulated or how it developed, but its popularity is certainly a signal triumph of the surface god. He delights in false reasoning and rightly considers all true syllogisms as blasphemies against him. He prefers propositions like this masterpiece of logical *non sequitur:* Exercise of the powers of the mind has led some religious to pride of judgment. Pride is the most formidable obstacle to union with God: He said that He rejects the proud. Therefore, since a good nun does not want to be proud, she must not think. To whatever lesser imperfections her frail human nature may succumb, let it never be said of her that she used her head.

Ludicrous as this sounds, there has scarcely been a more persistent heresy in religious life, and particularly in contemplative religious life, than the Heresy of the Head. It spawns a multitude of false notions, notably in the sphere of obedience. Now obedience is not less obedience when it is intelligent. A religious who is always perfectly submissive to her superiors, because she has meditated deeply on the meaning of authority and has come to understand that what is objectively preferable is not always preferable to God, and that to bow one's own judgment to the judgment of another can be in itself an act of good judgment, is an intelligent religious and a worthy religious. The nun who is always perfectly submissive to the judgment of her superiors because she never makes any judgments of her own anyway qualifies for neither accolade.

There is no particular need for professional scholarship in a cloister, though it is always useful. And secular scholarship is not normally to be pursued in a cloister of St. Clare. But the development of the power of thought is essential. We do not love better for thinking less. In the end, we love less. For we gradually settle down into being automatons. There is nothing admirable in living by reflex. We are not asked to answer the bell because the bell rang, but because the bell has reminded us of a particular thing God asks of us at the present moment. We obey when it is pleasant to obey with thanksgiving to God that our own ideas this time seem to coincide with His. We obey when it is difficult to obey because we have personally decided, with the power of intellect and will which God gave us, freely to submit ourselves to another's judgments, and have elected to do this thoughtfully and consciously as often as the need arises. If we do not obey in this manner, it is questionable whether we obey at all. More likely, we only take orders.

It has been said that no one likes to take orders. Does that statement really stand up under scrutiny? Is it not true that some persons *do* like to take orders, and precisely because they prefer a supine dependence which frees them from any personal responsibility for their own actions? The religious subject is a dependent, but this state of dependence has value only when it is intelligently and consciously assumed. The glorious paradoxical reward of this is that the nun who deliberately makes herself dependent on rule, dependent on superiors, is the only nun who is independent of the tyranny of self.

There are dozens of practical examples of how it is possible to live on the surface of one's own life when thinking has become a thing either suspect or rejected. The contemplative life is a life of faith. It demands a constant exercise of faith. Happily, this is a thing for which a woman is particularly equipped by the nature God gave her. Her knowledge is usually more intuitive than man's, which is more logical. She has a natural gift for piercing the surface of things and detecting their reality, for evaluating and comprehending symbols. If a postulant exercises and develops her natural womanly powers, she will come to understand more and more fully the meaning of objects, events, circumstances, situations, and individuals in the cloister. This is precisely, of course, what will make the surface god rend his robes in despair. His fond vision of life in the cloister is that tragic situation where minutiae become ends in themselves, customs wear steel braces against suppleness, and perfection defines itself as punctiliousness. When a religious woman falls into this trap, she is striking at the roots of her own womanhood.

Woman lacks many of man's characteristic qualities of mind and soul, but her grasp of symbol and her ability to sublimate what may appear detail into a kind of religious mystique not without validity is her own. It is one of her glories.

The month of December in a cloister is especially the season for a nun's exercising this womanly power and for plunging by faith beneath the surface of her own life. The bulletin board flutters with many more letters than usual these days, for the birthday of the Christ-Child arouses new confidence that prayers will be quickly heard. It would be a gross mistake, even an intolerable mistake, for a contemplative nun to see each letter stuck by a pin into the cork board as merely a request to be remembered in prayer, to "make the intention," and then go about her business.

Each letter is a separate *credo!* to be reverenced and appreciated as such. The worried mother whose daughter is engaged to the wrong kind of boy; the young doctor trying to build up his practice; the lonely old lady whose tenants won't pay and whose rheumatism is getting worse; the business man with the quarreling family; and the desperate woman whose letter is given central placing on the board: "Sisters, I am an alcoholic. I just can't overcome it. Pray for me, you are my only hope;"—all these people are saying the same thing in various ways: I believe in God. I believe in prayer. I believe in the worth of a life dedicated to prayer. And I believe such a life has meaning and value for me.

A nun must respond to their *credo* with her own, believing that her vocation obliges her to gather each of these people into her heart and her life. She is not committed to love either humanity in general or the community's benefactors in particular as a list, but as individuals. It is the perfectly normal development of her enclosed life that her heart expands to hold more and more of others' sufferings, more and more of their needs. It is not a question of reciting lists of names to God in prayer. Quite naturally, needs fit themselves into the program of her day; and while all needs and intentions must be carried always in her heart, the normal nun will experience repeatedly how this or that need will confront her at some small turning of her work or her prayer or her recreation.

The desire to lean restfully back in her choir stall at the night Office, let her breviary droop, and chant sleepily after a hard day's work loses all its urgency when the letter from the alcoholic again unfolds itself before her mind's eye: "Sisters, I get drunk every night over again. I can't control myself." No elaborate proofs need be brought forward to attest the fact that there is a mysterious connection between the tired nun who straightens up her sagging back, blinks back her sleepiness, and chants with every energetic ounce of her love, and the poor, sodden woman for whom she prays. If a nun does not understand this, she has not got beneath the surface of her vow of virginal chastity which commits her to the spiritual maternity of souls.

All these pre-Christmas days are super-busy days. Far from shutting out the world, they bring the world's problems closer.

When Sister Gabriel's irritation from a morning of constant interruptions of her work wants to blaze up into impatience, somehow the sorrowing father of that quarreling family intrudes himself on her gaze, and God may hear an aspiration of love instead of a sigh of annoyance. Sister Celine has her arms loaded with evergreens, and what if the needles *are* dropping on the floor Sister Stanislaus just swept? She is tired, and it is late, and how can she pick up the needles, anyway, with her arms loaded? Someone else will come along and pick them up. But there is that rheumatic old lady who would be happy just to be able to stoop. So Sister Celine delivers her evergreens and comes wearily back with the dustpan to retrieve the needles, knowing by faith that this is somehow availing for the old lady. All this comes just from getting under the surface of the letters on the bulletin board and thinking about what they mean and what they symbolize.

People bring their gifts to us at Christmas. Merely to be grateful for their charity is to stop short at the surface. Why do people bring gifts to nuns whose faces they have never seen, to whom they have never spoken? Why do these people consider enclosed nuns their particular friends? It is all a matter of faith. The people are giving testimony. The nuns are bearing witness.

When a poor couple purchase for mendicant nuns dainties they would never buy for their own family, a contemplative who has not stopped at a surface evaluation of her own life will not unduly bewail the poor spending their little store like this (though it will certainly add deep poignancy and humility to her gratitude), nor be greatly disturbed at thus occasionally having fare that scarcely qualifies as austere. She knows that these gifts are acts of faith in God, testimonials to the life of the spirit. It can be, after all, only because these people believe strongly in the value of a life given directly to God, believe in its value for them, that they come to offer these testimonials of love and esteem. Humbly to accept them as testimonials is to get beneath the surface of the vow of enclosure as well as the vow of poverty. If the nuns were not so willing to do without these things, probably people would not bring them.

When we are young in religion, we may yearn for rough and scanty fare even in holiday season. When we are older, we should have come to understand that at Christmas we eat not really cookies and fruitcake, but the acts of faith of our friends who sent them. And by these are nuns sustained. Contemplatives are called by God to live perpetually in a cloister so that they may bear witness to His sovereign supremacy. People bring them gifts as testimony that they understand the apostolate of the cloister.

Today we come in procession from the choir, and what gifts has the portress taken from the turn for us to see as we pass? There is the box of elegant fruit covered with cellophane, topped with a flaring satin bow. Next to it is a brown paper bag on which a large grease spot is growing larger. It holds a small and badly dented can of peanut butter. Gift of the rich, gift of the poor. Gift delivered by a uniformed errand boy, and gift brought to the monastery by the widow on relief who walked out with her can of peanut butter, beaming, to share her opulence with the nuns. "I got two cans," she announced to the extern Sister, "so I bring one for the Sisters."

The nun who does not pour out her love on the two, who does not eat the perfect pear as a prayer for the kindly rich, or who does not spread the peanut butter on her bread with humility before the largesse of the poor, has never understood her vocation. She has simply floated on its surface.

And there is the man who writes this Christmas to say: "Sisters, we have never been able to put anything by, but now we managed to save up $40.00 to put in the bank. So we are sending you $5.00. Pray for us." It would be an invincible dullard who would be merely grateful, and not also bow her head before so glorious an act of faith in God and prayer as that of the man who put $35.00 in one bank and $5.00 in another.

If the surface god goes into the church (which is a dangerous place for him to venture), he will see poinsettias flanking the altar and crib on both chapel and cloister sides. What are they?—bright splotches of beauty against curtained grille and straw-lined manger. The nun sees something entirely different. In the poinsettias from the Jewish architect and the ear specialist, the businesswoman in the city and the housewife down the road, she recognizes new acts of faith in the kind of life to which she has been called.

When St. Clare cautioned her nuns not to fall away by neglect or ignorance from the way of the Lord they had entered, "and thereby do a great wrong to so great a Lord, and to His Virgin Mother, and to our blessed Father Francis, *and to the whole Church, both triumphant and militant,*" she spoke as one who had certainly got beneath the surface of her own life and the life she desired her daughters to lead. She understood the repercussions on the entire body of the Church of a single contemplative nun's infidelity. She also makes it clear that she wants her daughters to think profoundly on their responsibilities, since she is at pains to point out that it is not only neglect but also ignorance which can make a nun's life superficial. St. Clare obviously did not subscribe to the Heresy of the Head, and knew that a cloistered nun has no right to expect people in the world to understand her vocation if she does not constantly strive to understand it better herself. To do this, she must think deeply and prayerfully not only of the meaning of life in general and the contemplative life in particular, but on every detail of her life.

Those outside cloisters who fall under the spell of the surface god need to think. They need to think about God, about eternal values, about what passes and what endures, about what is relatively important and what is intrinsically important. If they do this, prayerfully and with good will, the surface god will lose many a client.

Those inside cloisters who unconsciously float on the surface of their own lives need to think. They need to ponder the tremendous responsibility they take on by making solemn vows and living in the strict enclosure. It is, after all, the responsibility for the whole world and every soul in it they have elected to shoulder. Rather a job for any woman! They need to search beneath the appearances and symbols and increasingly discover the meaning of their lives. They need ever more consciously to assume their responsibility and to investigate what is required of them by God and society. They need to think deeply so as to equip themselves to be constant in routine and courageous in crisis, and especially thus to fit themselves for probing the mystery of their vocation with God's grace—which is promised not to the sleepers but to the vigilant.

The surface god would then throw up his hands in despair and sink beneath the waves.

4

The Top-Heavy God

There is this about God: we can never be sure what He will do next, but we can always be sure why He will do it. The reason will always be His love. The future He plans is hung with obscurity, but the love with which He plans every detail of it is the most manifest of all things and the most certain.

When we came to Roswell sixteen years ago, we were sure we had had our last train ride. Probably none of us would survive to go on another new foundation, so we were safe in our cloister walls now and forever. No one dreamed that only two years later, Pope Pius XII would issue his historic apostolic constitution, *"Sponsa Christi,"* and the vast machinery of the Church would go into motion towards the gradual setting up of federations of cloistered monasteries. We talked of this novel idea at recreation, but with the easy detachment of American nuns discussing the excellent plan the Holy Father had hit upon for helping cloistered nuns in Europe, or maybe in Africa, or perhaps in Indonesia.

The pope had written of the dangers of the complete isolation of monasteries, of situations where nuns were actually starving for lack of financial aid or lucrative work, of tiny communities struggling to preserve discipline and observance with a dwindling number of subjects and no recruits on the horizon, while other monasteries flourished in subjects and in means. These things, of course, did not happen in the United States. It was a good thing Rome was going to take care of countries where they did. Then, slowly, slowly, the larger story unfolded.

There was more to this thing than mutual financial aid and possible exchange of subjects, we discovered. There were such considerations as the preservation of primitive observance, of strict discipline, of a common interpretation of ancient rules and traditions. Then, at last, the full truth was borne in upon us. Rome wanted *all* cloistered monasteries federated into groups. Rome meant *us*, right here in Roswell where kindly people kept us supplied with cabbage and turnips, and where the Holy Spirit summoned vocations from distant parts.

It was December when a devoted and experienced friar came to call upon us and explain exactly why the Holy See wanted federations and what they would entail. This was Father Leo Ohleyer, O.F.M, appointed by Rome to guide the Poor Clares in the formation of a federation, and destined to become a brother indeed to his relatives in the Second Franciscan Order. He sat at our parlor grille that snowy morning of December 27 and explained to us what a federation means.

It is a great pity that well-meaning persons who persist in thinking that cloistered nuns must surely quiver with joyous expectation at the thought of getting out of the lock-up for a while could not have sat in on this interview between Father Leo and the Poor Clares. Yes, we could see the great benefit of a closer union of all our monasteries. By all means we wanted to do what the Holy Father so strongly recommended. But, Father dear, WE DON'T WANT TO GO OUT OF OUR ENCLOSURE. A sample of that morning's dialogue would run something like this:

Poor Clares: We like to stay in our cloister.

Father Leo: You won't have to go out except once in three years to attend the federal chapter.

Poor Clares: (soft moans) But that's so *often!*

Father Leo: Once in three years . . . (slight cough) Well, Sisters, only the abbess and the delegate you elect to represent your community at the chapter will have to go out. That's only two.

Poor Clares: (stern and unbending) Two are so *many*, Father! And our *abbess!*

Father Leo: (clears throat) The federal chapter will last only a week or two. They won't be gone long.

Poor Clares: (choral groan, full volume) A week or *two!* Oh! (protracted soft moan)

Father Leo: (blinks for a while) Well, Sisters, you can offer this sacrifice for the good of the Order. Remember, Rome wants it.

Father has now struck the sensitive chord. The lamentations die down. Father brightens. The Roswell Poor Clares are beaten. They vote unanimously to join the federation urged by the Holy Father.

Now perhaps no one but a cloistered nun can make much sense out of the jeremiads invariably called forth by the temporary exodus of one of their number. If the number grows to two, and one of the pair is the abbess of the community, the whole monastery wears a stricken air. An uninitiate who witnessed the departure of our abbess and delegate for the first federal chapter of Poor Clares held in Cleveland might have been tempted to jump toward one of two equally false conclusions: either these nuns are the most sentimental creatures on the planet; or, these nuns are slightly mad.

Admittedly, our farewell recreation gathering around our Mother and our delegate would have been appropriate for a pair of explorers setting out for Antarctica on a five-year dog-sled trip and facing probable death from exposure. Mother blinked back tears and Sister blinked back tears because they were going away. The other Sisters took out their handkerchiefs for the same reason. Mother Abbess was embraced and cautioned to keep her shawl on. Sister was embraced and threatened with dire reprisals if she did not write every day. And at this point the casual observer would surely have been excused for throwing up his hands and exclaiming: "My word! And they are only going for *two weeks!*"

Why, really, all the dramatics about a very brief excursion into the world? The answer will not fit into a phrase. It is part of an issue so large that it encircles the whole of cloistered community life. It needs a deep understanding of the contemplative vocation to comprehend it.

There is a great deal written in spiritual books about the trials of the common life. Canonized saints have said it was their mortification-supreme. Granted the premise that the common life is penance in top form anywhere, the conclusion about what it would mean to a score of women walled in a small space together until death do them part would seem sufficient to make strong men tremble. Without at all gainsaying the truth that the common life tests the soul's mettle as nothing else quite does, that it taxes patience and charity around the clock to live peaceably and graciously with temperaments that jar us and characters that strike sparks off our own, and granted that the most heroic if unspectacular virtue is required to fulfil the demands of the common life day upon month upon year, there is still another face to the situation. The joyous face, the rewarding face. Curiously, very little is written about *it*.

Whole books will be devoted to soothing counsels about how to bear with the ill-mannered religious, the bore, the meddler, and others of that inglorious company. And everyone has read how the Little Flower stood right there and let her thoughtless companion asperge her with dirty water in the laundry. Any mature religious has met all these people, and has gradually,—oh, so gradually!—even come to suspect that she herself is not always just a fragrant wayside flower blooming in the paths of her Sisters.

There will always be the nun who stomps down the creaking floor of the dormitory cloister just when the others are falling asleep, the one who flats on the high notes, the one who chants the Office just a little faster than everyone else, and the one who chants it just a little slower, the one who is always late, and the one who can't forego dispensing free advice on all matters. But all these nuns, like the situation, offer a double perspective.

These supposedly regrettable characters, along with that dreadful person who St. Therese drily remarks stole her best witticisms and put them out for resale as her own, have several other qualities which somehow get left out of the inventories in the top-heavy discourses on the common life. They are the same nuns who will leave their own work undone at real personal sacrifice to shoulder some of yours when you are overburdened. Their number includes the nun who trains an eye upon you in the laundry to forestall your lifting a heavy tub because she suspects your back is aching today, and the one who always remembers to tell you that the organ music at High Mass was really lovely, because she knows you practised hard and long at it. There is the nun who slips a note under your plate in the refectory to tell you how much she appreciates the Latin lessons, and there are nuns who always finish up the leftover-from-yesterday food at today's dinner so that the others get the fresh dishes. There are nuns who say an unthinking sharp word and are back in half an hour to swear they are not fit to live with, but would you,—anyway?

Any reasonably intelligent nun who has lived twenty years in a cloistered community should be able to qualify for a degree in psychology. She knows more about the foibles and the grandeur of human nature than many a man with degrees trailing after his name. Possibly no class of human beings lives so closely as enclosed nuns, if we exclude prisoners, whose case is different on a number of scores but principally because they are living together unwillingly, whereas cloistered religious come into this thing with open eyes, willing feet, and arms stretched out to embrace it. In fact, they have six years of training in enclosed living before they are qualified for permanent residence in the cloister.

It needs all this background to understand the grief a two-weeks absence causes. If common life is such a nightmare, why would two of the inmates feel entirely miserable at the prospect of escaping from it for a brief time? And should not the others rejoice that the sources of their trials were being reduced by two? There is nothing unreal or sentimental about the contemplatives' dread of separation. It simply reduces to a blunt fact overlooked in all too many books: nuns, who live more closely than does any other class of persons, really do, and in hard daily practice, love one another. We know one another all too thoroughly. But in the final reduction of terms, we find that the joys of the common life far outbalance its trials in number and in quality. And we suspect that the common life itself is part of the hundred-fold God promised to His religious, even in this life.

St. Clare has some quite striking words to confound those who would put her way of life down as hard and inhuman. "Let each one disclose with confidence her needs to another. And if a mother love and nurture her daughter according to the flesh, how much the more ought a Sister to love and nurture her Sister according to the spirit." This is a very broad permission given to nuns obliged otherwise to continual silence outside of recreation. Nurture them! Do not simply do chores for them or bear with their failings or perhaps pray for their conversion of manners (as they quite possibly may be praying with equal fervor for the conversion of yours), but feed them, nourish them, nurture them. Let those who come to tell you of their needs, their sufferings, or their problems find food at your heart's table. And when you yourself are in need, then knock at your Sister's door and humbly ask for the food of her understanding and help. No one is nourished on platitudes, and none grows fat on spiritual parsley. What can a cloistered nun feed her hungry Sister with, if not with love?

Woman's destiny is love. When she is loved, she is most completely herself, able to expand and unfold the riches of her being as a flower opens its full beauty only in sunlight. When she loves, she is exercising her great mission in life. And if love is the life work of all women, it is the particular vocation of the contemplative religious woman.

A cloister is, above all, a school of love. A postulant must bring an aptitude for love, the hallmark of her vocation. The rest of her cloistered life should be spent developing it. If she busies herself with this, she will not have to worry about developing her personality, peering at her psyche for evidence of possible neuroses, or speculating on whether her talents are being properly respected. In fact, she will not have the time. For love is a consuming fire. Its paradox is that when it consumes, it creates. What it consumes is every bit of dross, every superficiality and pretense, every camouflage. What it appears to create, but actually only reveals, is the core of the creature who is made in the image and likeness of God. God is love.

Love transfigures. This seems to be one of the things the top-heavy god of the common life does not take into account, but we have all had our own proofs of it often enough. I remember taking some group pictures home to my family during my high-school days, and being astonished when my mother pointed a finger at Vickie from another class. "What a pretty girl!" Mother said, "I don't think I ever met her." Now Vickie was, unfortunately, a most unlovable person, a gossip, a sharp-tongued faultfinder. It had simply never occurred to young me that Vickie was pretty. If it had, perhaps she might have been. On the other hand, when Mother once casually remarked that it was too bad Kate was so plain when her sisters were so attractive, I was outraged. Kate, plain! Why, Kate was beautiful. Kate was lovely. Kate was something to stop traffic. You see, I *loved* Kate.

It is not so difficult to penetrate the divine Mind on this point, either, if we multiply our finite powers of loving by infinity. Sober books sometimes inquire of us what God could possibly find to love in us, sinners, outcasts, derelicts from grace. It is possible to become so learned as to forget to be wise. For the answer to that inquiry is obvious, so obvious that certain writers seem to miss it or to dismiss it as too simple an answer for so profound a question. When shall we discover that simplicity is profundity, and go on to learn that the profound are very simple? Because God loves us, we are lovable and beautiful. "He hath first loved us." (1 John iv, 10)

His act of loving creates beauty in us. This wonderful, unplumbable thought becomes more and more fragrant with mystery as we grow older. It is what a poem for the anniversary of vows meant to say:

> I turn my face up to His face, and see
> How lovely I am grown for being loved.

In our small human measure, we, too, create beauty in those we love. Thus, the vocation of the contemplative religious woman, which is wholly and exclusively a vocation of love, is a vocation to create beauty. Her work is to make souls lovable to God, to make souls beautiful in his sight. Her first duty lies at home. And home in the cloister is a dwelling of very close quarters.

As we grow older, we marvel more and more at the things love discovers. "Love, and you will find love," said St. John of the Cross. We could add: "Love, and you will find beauty." Some untoward situation will rally secret forces in the nun who had before appeared so irritatingly unconcerned about things. That same situation will rip the attractive fringes off another and reveal unguessed shabbiness of spirit. A different situation will reverse these character and personality revelations of both parties. This is part of the mystery of the "holy community."

When I was a postulant, I was a little afraid of that frequently recurring term. On all formal occasions when a Sister addressed the community, she said: "Reverend Mother Abbess and holy community . . ." Thus she announced the Office of the day. In such terms the kneeling postulants and novices asked for the grace of reception. A nun even requested prayers for her departed parent in this way. And I kept worriedly turning over in my mind the increasingly remote possibility that I would be accepted into such sacred ranks. For I was very clear in my mind that I was not holy. When we postulants used to kneel each day in the refectory after dinner and chorus: "Reverend Mother Abbess and holy community, I beg for the grace to be received and for the holy habit," my imagination would summon up sad future days for the community when, in the event that I should get into this company at all, the formula for succeeding postulants would have to be: "Reverend Mother Abbess, holy community, and Sister X, I beg to be received." There would have to be this extra category for unholy me. Gradually, the realization took happy shape in my mind, however, that twenty nuns in a cloister are not necessarily twenty holy individuals, but that together they constitute a holy community. It is the community that is holy in the sight of God, despite certain obvious unholinesses of its members.

A religious community is a perfect little exposition of the doctrine of the Mystical Body of Christ. The patience of one supplies for the irritability of another. The latter's zeal is the lever for the pusillanimity of the former. Teresa of Avila was asked what she did when she saw what seemed manifest faults and failings in her companions. That most practical of mystics replied that she tried harder to practise the contrasting virtue. She added that charity consists in not being shocked, that charity is to practise the opposite virtue.

Thus, even our defects become a service to others. No amount of eloquent discoursing on self-effacement provokes us to practise it as does listening to someone else imposing her views. We most quickly learn to withhold our opinions until asked by seeing what an unlovely picture the one who constantly plunges in first and unasked creates. We are all such dullards since the fatal apple was consumed in Eden. And so we must often be taught negatively when we cannot learn positively. Humility never appears so desirable as when we are embarrassed by another's conceit. Silence under reproof is a very sweet goal when we hear the unbeautiful sounds of someone else engaged in a vigorous defense of herself.

It is all so wonderful. That the common life gives us not only so many positive joys of companionship, so many active incentives to virtue, but even teaches us by default.

Charles Lamb said that we cannot dislike anyone we really know. There may be certain individuals who at specified times would be inclined to think this must mean that we shall know some people only in eternity. Perhaps. Yet earthly life is full of revelations. We live day after day with persons who take us for granted and whom we take for granted. Each has her own concerns, her work, her salvation to work out, her perfection to let God chisel away on. And one unconsciously subscribes somewhat to the view that all men are islands in some sense of the term, insulated or at least peninsulated. Then the ordinary course of life is thrown out of joint. And yesterday's casual companions at recreation rise up and throw the whole strength of their virtue and the full warmth of their womanhood into the crisis. The meek find their voices, the gentle show their courage, the everyday companions become the valiant women ready to share with you the hard bread and the bitter waters. Often one of the really great rewards of a shattering sorrow is to see the splendor of others' virtue suddenly unveiled, and to feel the love of our ordinary daily companions closing in strongly and warmly around one. These are the times when one knows what a ridiculously top-heavy god chants the dirge of the common life.

In his bull of confirmation of the Rule of St. Clare, Innocent IV set himself to sanction "that form of life which the Blessed Father Francis gave you and you accepted of your own free will, and according to which you should lead a life in common, in unity of spirit and in the bond of most high poverty." These are familiar and facile phrases to any religious, perhaps so familiar as to escape any real attention.

Just what is unity of spirit? What, for that matter, is unity? And exactly what is spirit? The "let's get together" rally, the team spirit, the commercialized efforts for the common good can pass themselves off as unity; but twenty-five women in a cloister will need something a great deal sturdier than team spirit to hold them in the bond of unity which Clare of Assisi envisioned and realized.

When I was in high school, one of the typical meaningless but beloved yells which the cheerleaders used as a warm-up before the basketball games went like this: "All in together, girls! How is the weather, girls?—F I N E!" Maybe this is the picture well-disposed friends on the outside of the wall have of nuns in cloisters. Those who do not subcribe to the notion of the common life as something appallingly grim, fall into the opposite heresy. It is F I N E!

There is a great deal being written these days about how to "save" marriage. It seems that some persons have only just stumbled on a rock of revelation long hid from view: the man and wife should recognize their differences and accommodate themselves to each other! If it takes a great deal of putting down of one's personal views, a large measure of self-efface-ment, and a still more generous portion of tolerance to insure peace between two individuals whom we presume to be deeply attached to each other and whose future associates will be, so to speak, of their own making, what will be required of a score or more of Eve's daughters wishing to dwell under one roof forever, and desirous that the roof remain in place?

We come to the cloister unattached to one another, strangers. And the spiritual books plead with us to practise more and more detachment from creatures. Yet, all the time, what we need most is detachment from one creature only. I have waited for the book which would tell me what experience writes plainly enough: the thing to do is to get detached from yourself, and then you need never worry about getting attached to others. The deeper we plunge into the clean depths of this one detachment, the more rewarding is the common life. The more we love rightly, the clearer are the fallacies of the top-heavy god. We make gods of those we love wrongly, where God has forbidden us to have strange gods before Him. What we often call disillusionment is merely that a creature whom we have insisted should be a god has unmistakably revealed himself as a creature.

To love with consideration of creaturehood is to love without disillusionment, to love realistically, to love as a woman is made to love. A woman's nature is fashioned for observing little things. She is a creature destined for small services, little acts of fidelity, delicate thoughtfulness, persevering loyalty. In these very things is her greatness and her grandeur. Fidelity in smoothing over little rough ways for others, in receiving gratefully small services and becoming increasingly alert to perform them, in being quick to appreciate the little difficulties and embarrassments of others and to rejoice in their minor successes, is to transform the common life into a very rewarding affair whose joys enormously overbalance its sorrows.

So I was musing before the Lord on January 2 after that

historic December when we had cast our Roswell lot into the national federation of monasteries. It was that blessed fifteen-minute interval between collation and recreation when the choir always smells faintly of incense from the pre-collation holy hour, when only one dim bulb is burning and the sanctuary lamp licks at the darkness, and the Sisters squeak in and squeak out of the choir or proceed from station to station making the way of the Cross, squeak by squeak. There is asphalt tile in the cloisters and cells of the monastery. But in the choir and common room, there are wood floors. On the tile, the nuns walk silently along, betraying their approach only by a small jingling of beads. On the wood floors, their bare feet make small, delightful squeaks. I knelt there, looking at the figure of the Christ-Child lying on the first altar step in the simple manger Sister Leo had arranged. He is an unusual figurine. Not the darling doll of many a Christmas crib, this Infant has a slightly brooding expression. Instead of being tucked under his cheek or held up in aimless baby-fashion, these little plaster arms are stretched out full-length as though in a pathetic and tremendous effort to embrace everyone at once. Or as though waiting for nails.

And so we had begun another cloistered year. Yesterday we saw the New Year in, nun-fashion. We rose half an hour before the midnight Office, and knelt there silently in the choir until Mother Abbess gave the little sign. Thereupon we prostrated ourselves on the floor and recited the psalm *"Miserere"* in sorrow for all our sins of the dying year and for the sins of all people everywhere. But this could not be the end. No, then we rose to our feet and chanted the *"Te Deum"* in thanksgiving to God for all the love, all the joy, all the sorrow of the closing year. Next came the quaint and ancient ceremony when all the nuns file over to the abbess' stall and, kneeling before her, present her, each one, with a little New Year's greeting. Neatly folded over, the written message tells her of prayers that will be offered for her, the love felt for her, the thanks owed her. And Mother raises her hand in blessing over the bowed head of each daughter. Then each one kisses the abbess' hand in token of obedience. The two youngest postulants disappear into the tower and begin pealing the great bells. Another year has come. The midnight Office begins with a plea and a declaration of the work of the contemplative life: "O Lord, may You open my lips, and my mouth shall declare Your praise." A mouth declaring God's praise,—this is a cloistered nun summed up quite neatly. A mouth that declares His praise in the Office chants, or a mouth of the heart that loves.

That half hour before the New Year's Office is a hazy time. Memories of New Year's eve in so many past years come flocking into the drowsiness of the not-yet-quite-awake minutes. I recall the New Year's eve of my early teens and our first mixed party. That was back in the days when one was still a little girl at fourteen, and I remember how Jeanne and Helen and I found this new male company all very boring and finally retired apart to sit on the side of the bathtub and sing over the delicious harmony of our new three-part *Kyrie* for the school choir. This may possibly have been the one occasion in history when a *Kyrie* was rendered with such feeling from the side of a bathtub. And there was the New Year's eve just before I entered the convent, when Florence and I were making the year's-end retreat at the local retreat-house. Our little cottage was only a few yards from the chapel, but that was sufficient for me to step down into a snowdrift at midnight and come up with only one instead of two high-heeled pumps. I limped into the chapel on one black pump and one wet-stockinged foot, and wondered how things would be in the convent.

Now I know. Twenty years of rubbing souls with others in the cloister have convinced me that the top-heavy god is a fraud, stretching little annoyances to tragic lengths and hushing the little joys. January 2 of another year. "Squeak, squeak, squeak" I hear. And though I do not see her, I know that is little Sister Maria coming on her quick, even step. "Squeak, *SQUEAK*, squeak, *SQUEAK*" someone goes out. That is Sister Benedicta, who always steps lightly on her left foot and determinedly on her right. Twenty years of the closest possible living with some of these companions in the cloister, and some years at least with all of them. And I know each one's footstep as well as I know what the sudden ripple of Sister Dolores' left eyebrow means or the slight tightening of Sister Juliana's lower lip. And they know me, I am sure, quite as well. I place all the top-heavy pseudo-tragedies of the common life on the left side of the scale, and all the joyous rewards on the right. And as the right side falls down so heavily that the paltry things on the left are flung out and away, I put away my resentment that the federation is going to take two of us out of the cloister for two weeks every three years, bow my head before that wide-armed little figure on the altar step, and whisper to Him: "Lord, You know I love the very squeak of their feet."

5

More About the Top-Heavy God

In the fifteenth century God put some finishing touches on His Poor Clare work of the thirteenth century. That which Italian Clare and Francis had lovingly conceived and immortalized in what is probably the briefest of all monastic rules, French Colette insured and protected with constitutions. Exuberant Italian love and its singing idealism pervade the short rule of St. Clare. The logic and keenness of the French mind characterize the constitutions of St. Colette. Is it not entirely charming, the fact that the Assisian saints begged God for a Corbian saint when their seraphic ideal was fast losing its luster in many and many a monastery and friary of the fifteenth century?

There is something so canny in Italian Francis and Clare beholding from heaven with some trepidation (insofar as trepidation is compatible with bliss) what was happening to their Order on earth, and agreeing that what was needed to prop it up where it was sagging and to restore it where it had collapsed was French sanctity, sanctity characterized by sharp French insight and hard French practicality.

"Give us Colette!" St. Francis and St. Clare begged of God.

And God obligingly drew the French anchoress, Colette of Corbie, out of her anchorhold, gave her a friar for guide and companion, set her on a donkey, and despatched her through France, Belgium, and Germany to restore primitive Franciscan obsevance where it needed restoring. She did.

Especially noteworthy among the many practical reminders St. Colette supplies in her constitutions are those dealing with differences of persons. For example, she states flatly that you cannot lay down rigid norms about dispensations from the fast, remarking that "some are more enfeebled by a slight and passing indisposition than others are by a prolonged and grievous illness." Evidence of this abounds. One nun will be back at her post shortly after major surgery, bristling with energy, while another is struggling to drag along the aching limbs and hold up the pounding head her last month's cold left behind it. And the cruelest injustice is that pseudo-justice which is exercised in "treating all exactly alike."

I remember my short-lived basketball career in high school when I first plumbed certain profundities about the differences in persons. As freshmen, we were required to turn out for gym where, among other things, we were inducted into the mysteries of basketball, played according to boys' rules. The terminology alone was beyond my meager powers of comprehension in things athletic. "You can't walk with the ball," the coach cautioned us darkly; "you gotta keep dribbling." I thought this an obnoxious term, sounding perilously like drooling. So I mentally ruled out dribbling. Furthermore, the coach failed to point out that other variations of locomotion with the ball were likewise taboo unless one indulged in this thing called dribbling which I did not favor. So, with the prohibition against walking with the ball firmly in my mind, and having (probably by mistake) caught the ball thrown to

me by a trusting team member, I simply tucked the thing
under my arm and ran the full length of the gym to throw it
into the basket, a thing I found it considerably easier to do
when no one else was in the vicinity to trouble or distract me.
For when I set out on this historic run, I left nine players
behind me, rendered completely immobile by shock.

Instead of the colorfully concise instructions imparted to
me in public by a coach convinced that I had been let out
without my keeper, I sulkily reflected that I should have been
commended for running at all. Running had never been one
of my outstanding achievements. We had races at the school
picnics each spring during my grade school years, and the
only year I did not pant in last was the year that Ida Schmit-
zenberger fell down and twisted her ankle. So I was second
last. Now, in high school, I came up against this peculiar man,
the coach, and his quaint ideas about running being a way to
prepare for still more strenuous exercise. I personally considered running sufficiently exhausting to be held a terminal evil
rather than a preparatory one. But the coach had this strange
notion about running us at full pace twice around the big
gym, not in reparation for all our past sins, offenses and negli-
gences, but as a warm-up for the game.

The first time he sped us on this warm-up run, I retired to
the side at the end of the sprint and sat down. This seemed to
me the obvious thing to do. The coach thought otherwise. The
other girls were jumping foolishly about the middle of the
floor, awaiting further word, rubbing their hands and looking
disgustingly full of energy after the death run we had just
executed. "What are you doing?" the coach asked me. I pri-
vately thought this inquiry ridiculous, but being a product of
gentle rearing, I replied politely that I was resting after our
run. Now, I had always found the coach an extraordinarily

articulate man. It was a new experience to behold him speech-
less. After opening and closing his mouth several times with
interesting soundlessness, he finally said in a small, beaten
voice: "Listen, stop wearing an organdy blouse with your
gym suit, will you?" He added, almost pleadingly: "Nobody
wears organdy for basketball."

I was inclined to shrug at this. After all, there is no ac-
counting for taste. My mother had especially got this blouse
to go with the gym bloomers. It had ruffles on the sleeves and
a large bow on the collar, and mother said I looked very sweet
in it. But it is true that our livingroom mantel held no loving
cups won by my mother for her athletic prowess of former
years, nor had I ever known her to engage in any sport more
strenuous than checkers. And some fine womanly instinct told
me that the coach was a suffering, defeated man, not to be
reasoned with at that moment. So I forewent informing him
what my mother had said about how I looked in organdy.

This childhood memory has recurred to me many times in
the cloister. A coach who could not understand that most
girls' fun was some girls' misery has his conventional counterpart in many of us who do not understand that what causes
anguish to one nun may be a matter of no concern to another.
And that is just where the top-heavy god can start proselytizing from the other direction. He enlarges his clients' personal difficulties and inflates their sense of how well they are
carrying them off. He diminishes the trials of others and suggests that they certainly do not know how to suffer and endure. His achievement is always the creation of an atmosphere. In this case, it is an atmosphere of, "I put up with so
much, I do so much; and heavens! how that one does exag-
gerate! How this one does fail to cooperate! How immature
she is, letting such small things trouble her like that. She does
not know anything about real suffering."

None of us would be quite so monstrous or quite so honest as to phrase the idea as crudely as that, but the idea exists independent of syntax. And it implies that there is a measuring rod for suffering, that a given trial produces a given reaction and exacts a given toll of any two or any dozen nuns. If Sister Paschal and Sister Assumpta are misunderstood and wrongly blamed, then Sister Paschal and Sister Assumpta should feel the same twinge, gulp the same brave gulp, and come up in the same specified time with the same victorious smile. When Sister Dolores and Sister Stanislaus have had the flu, it is obvious that when Sister Dolores has recovered, Sister Stanislaus must have recovered, too.

These examples sound ridiculous, and they are ridiculous. Yet, we live by very ridiculous standards once we have given the least grain of incense to the top-heavy god. These things happen everywhere, but they are more immediately fatal in the cloister where life is lived in such close quarters. The first time I ran up sharply against the tremendous differences in character and personality which must be taken into particular account in a cloister, I was a very young postulant.

One day I was a little late for recreation, having had to finish up a small chore. To miss any of the hilarity of a novitiate recreation was, of course, a thing bordering on tragedy. So I came bounding down the stairs and around the bend of the hall with more enthusiasm than decorum. And I stumbled directly onto another black-caped postulant. Laura had her hands over her face and was crying softly.

Now, at nineteen, most of us are more forthright than subtle. So I demanded at once: "What's the matter? Did someone die?" Laura shook her head. I was casting about for the next query on my list of possible tear-provoking eventualities, when Laura began backing away. I reached for her hand. "What are you doing out here?" I pursued. After all, I was a veteran postulant of several monastic months, with what I then considered corresponding rights to investigate such odd occurrences as this. Laura had entered only a week before, but evidently she understood the self-invested authority of a senior postulant. "I can't go in there." She gestured toward the novitiate common room from which giggles and a confusion of tongues were just then simultaneously issuing. I stared at her and dropped her hand. Laura must have taken this for a withdrawal of sympathy, for her tears ran faster. "I never know what to say," she stammered miserably. "I can't ever think of anything to say. And they will expect me to say something. They will all look at me." I shall never forget the impact of the education I received in that moment. We were two young postulants standing together outside the novitiate at recreation, I all eagerness to get inside and swell the chorus, Laura overcome at the appalling prospect of entering that roomful of mirth.

I looked at her thin little face with the tear lanes curving down it, and felt suddenly very small before a sorrow I had never dreamed existed. "You'll have to go in," I whispered; "they'll miss you." Something with dark wings flew through Laura's eyes, so I added hastily: "Listen,—we'll go in together. I always talk so much at recreation, if you just stay next to me and laugh once in a while, they will think you are talking, too." There was certainly nothing in this sage solution to solicit any response from Laura except that she must have sensed its very real compassion. It could only have been that suffering Laura understood that, for all my clumsiness, I was really suffering with her, that she stopped crying and looked at me. That day began a great friendship.

Superiors are urged to be understanding of their subjects, but this is not enough. Subjects must be understanding of subjects. And this cannot be superficial. When we deal with any human being, we are in the presence of a great mystery. No one has ever penetrated a mystery by lowering the head and charging through it. Yet, this is precisely what unsound psychology would have us do: force doors open, make interminable inquiries, drag out confidences, and then—prescribe. If twenty years of cloistered living has taught us anything at all about human nature, it should have taught us to be humble in our understanding, though this is admittedly not a field where the importance of humility is often urged.

The doctrine of any false god is always some form of extremism. It could not be otherwise. For balance is of the true God. Balance is humility, a thing for which no false god has ever been distinguished. The top-heavy god specializes in extremism simply by reason of being the top-heavy god. So his unwary clients will either give a snap of the mental fingers, as indicated above, for the sufferings of others; or, they will unpack their do-it-yourself psychiatric kit and go to work at "understanding" a companion with all the determination of a rivetter and just as much delicacy.

Actually there should be no one thing more humbling in life, and particularly in religious life, than the discovery of how little we understand those with whom we associate so intimately. There is always a rightness in humility. And there is rightness here. We ought to be humble before these mysterious beings around us, each with her own burden of spiritual experience for wealth or poverty, her hereditary urges, her past environmental conditioning, her educational shaping, and, more profoundly, her individual complexus of mystery. All that makes each person unique must summon our most humble respect. Not to respect uniqueness is already to have disqualified oneself for ever understanding a human being. It is in this way that the extrovert deplores the sensitiveness of the introvert, and the introvert is secretly scornful of the insensitiveness of the extrovert. Thus two persons fail each other, and each fails herself; where two persons might have contributed gloriously to the fulfilment of each other.

The point is not to ferret out the mysteries of another's personality, but to wait humbly outside the portals in case one might ever be needed inside. It is a false and devouring love that seeks to pick the locks of another's soul, but it is a humble and detached love which observes and waits at the door. When we see a companion suffering at a remark, an incident, a circumstance, we should emerge from the experience considerably wiser. We know what wounds her; and if we have any sense at all, we usually know why it did. We therefore understand her better. And, presumably at least, we understand better how not to inflict similar pain. In the close confines of the cloister, such lessons must be taught, learned, digested, and coordinated into other experiences with exquisite delicacy until they have become part of our spiritual fabric.

But, what if we are not delicate? Then, we are to become so. Each new year of living under God's name, daring to accept the title "spouse of Christ" should certainly bring progressive refinement. A nun who becomes coarser in her dealings with others as the years pass, instead of increasingly refined, is testifying to her failure as a religious. It is possible, especially in the tight quarters of the cloister, to come to "take others for granted" in the sense that we expect them to bounce back like good tennis balls from our crude tossings of their opinions, sensibilities, and problems. But it is a possibility that should make us quail. It is indeed a tragedy to arrive at that peak of self-complacency from which we dismiss the suffering of those whose suffering differs from our own, the ideas of those whose opinions do not coincide with ours, with a facile labelling of "immature." The best way to insure a permanent state of unripeness in oneself is to consider oneself fully mature. We are always learners. And everyone with whom we live is our teacher, in one way or another.

Suffering cannot be weighed, nor classified as to worth. Laura in her agony of shyness and someone else in her blustering boldness cannot be successively set on the spiritual scale, weighed and tabulated—with a prognosis indicated.

G. K. Chesterton, who was a poet and therefore equipped to be more a friend than a warden of lunatics, delivered a superb compliment to the hero of his own novel, *The Poet and the Lunatics,* when he wrote of Gabriel Gale's humble endeavors to understand all; how if a man insisted that Gabriel was made of glass, Gabriel would try his best to appear transparent. This would make a magnificent ideal for any Christian, more particularly for religious, very specifically for cloistered religious who ought by reason of their vocation to be or to become specialists in understanding.

To attempt an explanation or to venture a shy confidence, only to be met with the emphatic reply: "I simply do not understand you at all," is often to render this the person's last attempt and final venture. It is very possible that one person's suffering, problem, or confusion is as alien to the experience of another as glass to stone. But we can always pray for the grace to feel transparent. How different it is to say: "I wish I understood you better. Could you help me?" rather than immediately to dismiss the unfamiliar as the unimportant or to confuse it with the unrealistic.

In the sphere of suffering, reality is relative and subjective. The hardest reality in spiderdom is a fragile web, and even the dullest spider knows it. To the ox, a spider web would scarcely constitute a formidable reality. To human beings, it is a symbol of fairyland. While the human society is restricted in membership to human beings, there is still a valid analogy.

To say that it is humbling to realize on occasion or in a crisis how little we have understood those with whom we live is not to contradict the truth of cloistered religious knowing one another so very, very well. In fact, it is an extension of that truth. We usually know and can even foresee reactions, we see the small failures and sometimes are delicate enough to notice the little successes. We vibrate to overtones of a voice and react to a fleeting expression. These things come automatically with the passage of years. But humbly to enter the mystery of another's life is a thing for which our very knowledge of our companions sometimes most unfits us.

We can know people so well as to delude ourselves into thinking that we understand them. And so we fail to humble ourselves before them. We become druggists filling prescriptions, not specialists in the field of delicacy.

Years ago when I had the educational delight of watching that superb showman, the late Daniel A. Lord, S.J., direct his "Matrimonial Follies," I thought I was responding merely to the techniques of a master both of theatre and of humanity. He would stride up and down the aisles of St. Louis University Theatre, the old white sweater worn in his unique fashion, spread across his back and its sleeves tied under his chin. He would chide, shout, grin, approve, always and precisely where chiding, shouting, grinning or approval were needed. I was so fascinated that I did not even die, as one would be expected to die at seventeen, when my hoopskirt hooped.

We were wearing evening dresses for the chorus, and that was when hoop petticoats were popular for evening. It was my first, and I had had no experience in taming a hoopskirt. I sat down. The hoop stood up. But Father Lord only smiled, and with one quick wave of the hand had us all stand up again. It was such a little thing, but I keep the memory in with the faded little newspaper picture of him in our breviary, the picture with the caption: "Jesuit dies of cancer." It is a spur to recollection to turn to the *Benedictus* Canticle and see the smile of a man so understanding because he was so humble. He moved among us callow youngsters never as a superior being, but as our companion. He brushed aside our smartness, our crudeness, our colossal conceit, and smiled his wonderful smile on the idealism, the unsureness, the secret shyness of the young. And so we loved him.

I remember him at the summer schools of Catholic Action he sponsored in different cities each year for his sodalists. Nor was I too young to observe how his apparent casualness kept sharp eyes for any least suffering. I have seen his valuable time wasted by bores so famous that those less great and less humble than Father Lord would have beat a lightning retreat at their approach. But he smiled, a genuine smile. And he listened, really listened. I think he learned a great deal, even from the bores. At the evening of dancing in the hotel ballroom where the summer schools were held, after a day of sessions in spirituality, Father Lord was everywhere. He never failed to notice a neglected girl standing apart. He always knew how to dash a too-smart boy's remarks on the rock of his own good humor. And then he would jump up on the bandstand, clap his hands loudly, and announce: "Time for night prayers." Immediately, several hundreds of young people would kneel down on the dance floor and say night prayers together. He made it seem the most natural way in the world to end a dance.

I went off to the convent with my bright little horde of memories of Father Daniel Lord, the man everyone loved, the priest with a million friends—genial and smiling, master of every situation. After his death from cancer in 1955, a death welcomed with the same blitheness that had characterized his life, I learned about some of his suffering: the backwash of his tremendous powers of loving which made it seem intolerable for him to know himself vigorously unloved by even a very few. The priest who could not bear to let a lonely girl bloom as a wallflower felt dislike of himself so keenly that he could not without great effort be "himself" in a group that held someone out of sympathy and at odds with him.

After my first youthful start of surprise that so lovable a man could be unloved by anyone, I began to realize that was *why* he had understood people so well. That was why he had loved bores and nuisances, smart alecks and wiseacres, as well as the charming and attractive. He had suffered acutely himself from occasional lack of love and understanding. And suffering had enriched him. It is a good thing to remember, and wonderfully encouraging, that this gayest of neighborhood saints understood out of being misunderstood, and loved without boundaries because of being himself sometimes unloved.

A nun who nestles down into her own sufferings would witness a natural phenomenon if she were not too occupied with her nestling process to witness much of anything. The phenomenon is that of personal sufferings dilating themselves to heroic size. Nestled in them, however, she obviously cannot get outside and discover other perspectives on suffering. Perhaps this is what most often accounts for the top-heavy god's success in proselytizing. When we are all curled up in our own sorrow—real, inflated, or imagined—the doctrine of the top-heavy god takes on a very orthodox ring. *Eheu mihi!*—but not quite as the psalmist meant.

The treatises which the top-heavy god inspires on the anguish of the common life have a way of overbalancing themselves, urging the gentle reader to bear with the faults of others in a manner which strongly suggests that the gentle reader herself offers others nothing to be borne with, and especially that she has nothing to bear with in herself. The shrewd author of the *Following of Christ* had a different outlook. "And how shall you expect to have others to your liking, since you cannot make your own self as you desire?" (Bk. I, ch. 16) The subtler invasions of the top-heavy god, though, are his false levellings of individuals and situations. He is top-heavy with his one idea: *I*, out of proportion, out of perspective, and inevitably out of joint with others.

The homespun psychologists in a cloister know just about everything that everyone else does or says. Very often, it takes years before one of them has attained enough humility and practised sufficient patience to understand *why* another nun does what she does or says what she says in the way that she does it or says it. Respect for human dignity is something more than respect for the right to life and its endurance, something greater than the admission of basic rights common to all, something eclipsing courtesy and forebearance. It is something that probes the very mystery of creaturehood. Probes, that is, if it is allowed or invited.

Much suffering is caused in life inside and outside cloisters by positive misunderstanding and the negative lack of understanding. But a far subtler harm is done by "understanding" others,—whether they like it or not! One of pride's most insidious forms is this kind of "understanding"; that is, the assessment of another creature by one's own standards, taking his measure with one's personal spiritual yardstick, and labelling him with one's own handy tags. Maybe there are too many complaints about misunderstanding. After all, we are meant to be misunderstood. We are all mysteries of God's love, private revelations of His wisdom. Mysteries must always remain at least partially veiled. Private revelations are not for instant and universal consumption. To be completely and exquisitely understood at all times by even one person could well be a real obstacle to union with God. Ultimately, we are the Lord's.

Conscious of the mystery of personality, we shall learn from it, be humbled by it, and often be rejoiced at its partial unfolding. And we shall never attempt to unhinge it so that we can study its component parts. Every joy in our own life should increase our capacity to rejoice with others. Each heartache, body-ache, or soul-ache of our own should equip us to compassionate the aches of others with greater delicacy. "Rejoice with them that rejoice: weep with them that weep," advised St. Paul. (Rom. xii,15) This lies at the heart of all communal living. It *must* lie at the center of cloister living, which is communal life in the closest possible quarters. And the apostle's further remarks are even more apposite: "Who is weak, and I am not weak? Who is scandalized, and I am not on fire?" (2 Cor. xi,29)

Often the most delicate office of love is not to be strong in helping the weak, but simply to be weak with the weak. We all prefer being loved on the plane where we are, however low and flat it is, rather than to be reached down to by a superior sort of being from a higher altitude. It is noteworthy that the only thing the dwellers in high altitudes usually bring to another's need is platitudes. God Himself showed us the right way, "Who being in the form of God, thought it not robbery to be equal with God: but emptied himself, taking the form of a servant." (Phil. ii, 6-7)

This is the whole secret: to empty ourselves. It is the formula for happiness in cloisters and out of them, too. It is why Father Daniel Lord had such power over young people. It is why a nun whose other imperfections may be obvious enough can still inspire and encourage and rejoice her companions. Reversely, it is why the top-heavy god is so top-heavy. He cannot empty himself of that one big idea of his which is: I.

It is February now, the quiet interval between the jubilation of Christmastide and the austerities of Lent, an ideal time for making reassessments and doing any spiritual recharging indicated. It is especially a beautiful month to be married in. That is what petite Sister Maria is going to do on the fourteenth, which happens to be a special day in the Franciscan Order, the feast of that St. Colette with whose story this chapter began. It is also the feast of St. Valentine, the day which all the Christian world associates with love. And because Sister Maria is going to make her first vows on that day and hear Holy Church officially call her the bride of God, there are great things astir in the novitiate. Flutes must be played and organs must sound; there must be a fierce cleaning and pitiless scrubbing of everything in sight. Sewing machines must hum to the tune of a new veil and guimpe and cord. And there must be and will be great joy everywhere, as the very different children of the community close in with love around the one of their number who is so loved by God as to have Him accept her vows.

Different indeed . . . responsible little Pauline with the golden hair, Linda with the biggest dimples in the southwest and that determined expression, Therese with the laughter of morning and the enthusiastic stride, Sister Maria herself, queen of this particular February, with her dainty manners and thoughtful eyes. Mysteries all, and caught up by God's love into the mystery of the contemplative life where the top-heavy god can be a menace only if he is not consistently knocked over. It is not so hard. He is top-heavy. Merely a determined push will do it.

6

The Hyperopic God

Then, suddenly, it was March. And the federation of Poor Clare monasteries which Father Leo Ohleyer, O.F.M., had explained to us last December was to be officially inaugurated. The first federal chapter would be comprised of the various abbesses and one delegate from each monastery, and was to be held in Cleveland at the Poor Clare monastery there. The leavetaking foretold in chapter three was now a reality. Not only our abbess and our delegate were occupied with many speculations about going off to Cleveland. All of us were.

It *is* rather strange, come to think of it, never to have met your closest relatives. For centuries, abbesses of Poor Clare monasteries have corresponded, exchanged ideas, asked advice of one another. For just as long, the nuns in each monastery have loved to hear about the nuns in all the other monasteries of the Order. That they should see one another was, however, a thing beyond the limits of possibility. For, we never go out! And that is just the accusation two dear old ladies on the San Francisco Chief were to level against Mother Abbess and Sister Anne when they spied them.

Sister Anne was elected our delegate because, according to her, she had the basic requisite qualities, being just old enough for the job and still young enough to swing into an upper berth with ease. But it seemed so unreal to the rest of us that we now had somebody called a delegate who went off to the Cleveland house, our oldest monastery in this country, to represent the thought of the Roswell Clares on observance, discipline, and anything else that might happen to be mentioned. We looked at the official document from the chancery hanging on the bulletin board which told us that Archbishop Edwin V. Byrne was allowing Reverend Mother Abbess and Sister Anne to leave the enclosure to attend a federal chapter in Cleveland. We cast hostile glances at the open suitcase up in St. Joseph's room, half-packed with nuns' necessaries like Mother's alarm clock and Sister Anne's Latin grammar. Unlike the ecumenical council, the federal chapter was not to be conducted in Latin, but Sister Anne intended to use any spare moments on the train to prepare the next few Latin classes. The vernacular will be warmly welcomed at the front door of the monastery if the Church wants it, but Latin studies with the richness of intellectual and spiritual development they contain will not be ushered out the back.

And so we waved our travellers out of the enclosure doors on a sunny day in early March, with mixed emotions about federations. Our extern Sisters, Imelda and Colette, swept Mother and Sister off to the station and efficiently saw to all the mysterious processes connected with getting the big suitcase on to Cleveland by way of the baggage car and seeing that the lunch box did not get into the baggage car. Then the train pulled out of the Roswell which nine of us had pulled into with the conviction that we would never leave it again.

The monastery is very auspiciously situated as regards departing nuns who want one last look at their cloister before chugging off into uncharted worlds. The property lies fairly close to the railroad, just outside the city limits. Ten minutes after leaving the station, the travellers again caught sight of their home, looking like a faintly pink dollhouse in the distance. Mother Abbess and Sister Anne waved sadly and ineffectually at the monastery, and took out their handkerchiefs, though for purposes more immediately practical than waving. The conductor started down the aisle to check the tickets. "Dry your eyes," hissed Mother Abbess sternly to Sister Anne, "he'll think we are being put out of our Order." The force of this command was somewhat weakened by the fact that Mother was in need of her own handkerchief, but Sister Anne wisely decided to forego any comment to that effect.

Then the two little old ladies advanced to take their private census. What Order? Going where? What for? Four grey eyebrows shot up at the confession that the nuns were Poor Clares. There was a short whispered conference, and smiles faded into a somewhat suspicious pursing of the lips. "Poor Clares never go out," old lady #1 reproached the travellers. Old lady #2 produced references: "I read a book about them. They can never get out." Sister Anne heroically forswore the temptation to reply: "Well, it's not easy, ma'am; we made a break for it." It seemed better to leave the situation to Mother Abbess, who coped with it in her usual effective fashion.

Cloistered nuns out of cloister must have an especially stranded look about them, for the more they endeavor to lose themselves in the anonymity of train chairs, the more are some kind people determined to cheer them. An old gentleman across the aisle who looked the last person to strike up conversations with strangers, surveyed our pair for some time with covert glances. Finally he cleared his throat, respectfully removed his hat, and astonished the two with his query: "Would you like to hear some really keen Texas jokes?"

To others, however, any nun is reckoned to be equal to any situation. Up forward, a plump infant began to cry. The young mother bounced him and cooed at him to no avail. A soldier in the middle of the car unwound himself from his remarkable napping position, legs that terminated in feet of formidable size hoisted in air, and strode up to the mother. "Here, give him to me; I'll take him back to the Sisters." Sister Anne mourned the fact of being the only one of us to behold Mother Abbess with a stranger's crying baby set down on her lap without further preamble.

Everyone wants to help nuns, and Sister Anne told us of her reflections about those who want to liberate modern religious from wearing habit, guimpe, and veil. Without the religious garb, our travellers were merely an elderly woman and a young woman. With it, they were religious ladies for whom soldiers carried suitcases, men tipped respectful hats, ladies smiled and bowed, and whom children excitedly saluted.

A young Negro saw Sister Anne looking longingly at the small but heavy suitcase slung up into the luggage rack above her head. "I'll lift that down, Sister," he volunteered. Sister gratefully extracted her breviary and watched the gallant young man swing the suitcase up again. In Elida, more glances indicated a new need. It was swung down again by the dark cavalier, Kleenex removed, and the suitcase swung back. In Portales, it became clear that the Latin grammar could be managed at this slow roll of the train. Down with the suitcase, out with the grammar, up with the suitcase. In Clovis, the young man looked abject and said apologetically: "Sister, I have to get off now." Sister Anne said she felt he feared she would reply: "Well, really, of all the nerve!"

It is a very strange feeling to arrive at a monastery fifteen hundred miles from one's own. Here live the people you have known for years by letter, but never seen. What will it be like in another cloister? The same rule, the same constitutions, yes. But, after all, each monastery is autonomous and completely independent. It receives its own postulants, invests its own novices, professes and then, considerably later on, buries its own nuns. With the physical isolation of centuries between us, how could we hope to find any other cloister much like the Roswell cloister, women being famous as they are for originality in the smallest matters?

Mother Abbess and Sister Anne were met at the station and unloaded at the Cleveland monastery by the obliging parents of our Sister Maria who lived there, the hour being too late for the Cleveland extern Sisters to be out. They crossed the driveway on which snow was still falling and mounted stairs that looked very bleak in the midnight cold, with a certain feeling of "alas!" The crocuses and hyacinths had been blooming back in Roswell.

But then two of the extern Sisters appeared in the door with smiles that extended well back into their wimples. "Welcome! We are *so* glad to see you." Faintly cheered, Mother Abbess and Sister Anne moved to the two big doors marked "enclosure." The doors were thrown open to reveal the beaming abbess of the Cleveland house, flanked by her beaming vicaress and the beaming portress. The two abbesses surveyed each other for five seconds or so, and then fell upon each other in the warm embrace of blood sisters reunited after long years of separation. Sister Anne was gathered to Mother Vicaress' heart. The portress hustled suitcases out of the way expertly. And Mother Abbess and Sister knew they might not be in Roswell, yet they were home.

As abbesses and delegates from Virginia to California assembled, the tenacity with which enclosed nuns in general cling not only to rule but to custom became evident in matters encouragingly large and delightfully small. We had wondered how vast the differences in interpretation of regulations and customs between Roswell and the other monasteries would be. Mother Abbess and Sister Anne now fell to marvelling at how negligible the differences were.

There is something strangely moving in hearing abbesses and nuns from far-flung monasteries, who have never seen each other before, speak in the selfsame graceful old terms of monastic address, to see them fold the familiar checkered table napkins in exactly the same way, to discover the very same small practices of monastic poverty. It is in their fierce love of their heritage that contemplative nuns are strong in unity and unshakable in loyalty. And this love has kept intact small usages to the extent that the federal capitulars can assemble from so many different states and find themselves bound in unity of manners as well as of ideal.

In every virtue, however, there can be a seed of error. Heresies have been founded on Gospel passages out of context. And always in our greatest strength lurks our weakness. For enclosed nuns of any Order, this can be an unrecognized allegiance to the hyperopic god, the god who sees so well at a distance but so poorly in close surroundings. And the hyperopic god who stalks cloisters is always looking back over his shoulder at the past. His farsighted vision is, therefore, also rear vision.

What is so patent in many quarters in the Church today could not fail to be patent in cloisters where mistakes, when they occur, must necessarily occur in a concentrated form. Loyalty to the Church can define itself in the practical business of living as an almost absolute refusal to see what is happening around us because of looking so fixedly at the past. Loyalty to her centuries'-old rule may cause a nun to develop a blind spot for the present because she is staring with such farsighted vision—backwards. Generalizations are never fair, but it is necessary to generalize to some extent in anything but a purely statistical survey, which the reflections here do not pretend or aspire to be. And, generally speaking, there can be no doubt but that nuns are often inclined to reject new ideas.

It is very understandable. Their roots have been put down so deeply in the past. Their spirit is that of a saint who lived centuries ago. Their heritage is venerable. Their rule is ancient. All this is to the good. It veers to the bad only when nuns forget that a spirit is a living thing. It leans to the very bad when nuns fail to reflect that an Order which is not supple enough to bend with the time is a dead weight on the Church and on society. Part of the glory of federations is their function of correcting rear farsightedness. The hyperopic god really finds federations quite detestable.

Let us take the case of St. Francis and St. Clare. They were very obviously children of their century. They spoke the language of chivalry. They loved their own age and immortalized in their rules and by their lives all that was best in it. They also knew the weaknesses of their particular age, and fortified their sons and daughters against them. St. Francis would not have his friars handle money because he saw all too many avaricious monks and prelates around him, and preferred a drastic prevention to a dubious cure. And, in his age, he proved it was quite possible for friars to live and fulfil their ministry in the Church without handling money. His principle will never be outmoded. But in the twentieth century, the method of acting on it cannot be the same as it was in the thirteenth.

He forbade his friars to ride horseback, because the rich

travelled so; and friars minor were poor men. He did not prohibit Cadillacs. Would he not, however, prefer his friars to "break the rule" and prefer a horse to a Cadillac today? Or, to be a little more realistic in our example, a Chevvy to a limousine?

Men do not ordinarily have a great deal of trouble with this matter of adaptation of a religious rule, though Vatican II has made manifest that adaptation in the Church is a problem for some of them, too. Women, however, excel in having trouble of this kind. Enclosed nuns are only true to their species when they are tempted to squirm at change. Temptation, of course, and capitulation are two very different things. And here is a happy case of: federations to the rescue!

St. Clare said that the nuns who cannot read their Office are to say instead the *Our Father* a specified number of times for each canonical hour. And she cautioned those who did not know how to read that they should not be anxious to learn. This is readily understandable counsel to women of her time by a woman who was privileged to be educated as relatively few women then were. It was also very wise advice by a woman who was doubtless canny enough to know that there could well be some who would enter medieval cloisters, if not for the sole purpose of learning the three r's, at least to get grounded, free of charge, in the first two. Yet, it would be preposterous for her progeny to allow scruple and puzzlement, anxiety and timidity, to arise out of this candid counsel of a shrewd thirteenth-century abbess and begin to fear there is something wrong about learning in general. Consequently, the daughters of Clare sort out her ageless meaning from words specific to a century and a situation.

We have noted that seven centuries ago St. Francis said the friars should not handle money. No one worries that a Franciscan friar today is not the right sort of friar because he has a quarter for bus fare in his pocket. The founder's ideas have been adapted to our times. Just so are St. Clare's adaptable to our age. No girl would be received in any of her cloisters today who could not read. And the postulant who does not learn to read better and better will have to deal with the Mistress. Consequently, there should be no hesitation to carry through this idea and encourage the modern postulant just out of her high-school or college classroom, her office, or her apartment, to study the deeps of the Divine Office, to which so great a part of her life will be given.

The old idea of a nun standing in her stall and chanting words she does not in the least understand, and has no business understanding anyway, does not find favor with a modern girl. It should not. To be "God's little trumpet" is no longer an ideal. For a nun is not a little trumpet. She is a living being set in a cloister to worship God in spirit and in truth. It is not alarming that she should like to know what she is talking about. It would be very alarming if she did not.

Only sixty years ago, a full high-school education for a girl was something to set her apart. It is now common to all. Fifty years ago, a college education for a girl was a rare phenomenon. It no longer is. Where formerly a girl had everything arranged for her from her wardrobe to her husband, girls now arrange things for themselves. The triumph of proper home environment and valid education is not that their alumnae should be incapable of independent thought, but that they should be able to steer their own courses. And this is something to be turned to spiritual advantage in the cloister as elsewhere, not a state to be mentally clubbed out of the subject until her concept of obedience has shrunk from childlike candor to complete childish dependence. We are responsible for our own actions, obedience or no. And the nun who is most consciously responsible for hers is, in the end, the most obedient.

It requires no wrench of the imagination to picture a St. Clare who happened to be born in the twentieth century, instead of the thirteenth, gathering her nuns around her to investigate certain passages of the day's Office, to delight in the rich poetry of a hymn. She consoled her nuns that they could always get something out of any sermon if they set their minds and their jaws to it; but still she tried to get the most learned as well as the holiest friars to speak to her daughters whenever she could. It is not at all necessary for modern contemplatives to become erudite exegetes, but it is certainly necessary for them to understand more and more deeply the great work of their lives, the Divine Office.

St. Colette, in the first draft of her constitutions, did not favor the study of Gregorian chant. Why? Obviously not because she considered the Church's most sacred music too frivolous for contemplatives, nor because she was tormented with fears that a nun who could distinguish an oriscus from a quilisma might get ideas in her head and come to an evil end. Her point was most probably made in the name of seraphic poverty. Vellums and parchments of Gregorian music were rare and extremely costly. Bound books of sacred music would be well beyond the category even of collector's items as far as mendicant nuns were concerned. How different when today's postulant enters the cloister. As surely as her Uncle Horace gets her a black umbrella (which she won't need anyway) does the pastor offer to get her a *Liber Usualis,* which she will need.

If there is no scrupling about this, neither should there be about the postulant being taught the theory of Gregorian chant and maybe getting downright scholarly about it after a while, too. Why should there be? Surely, if anyone should sing intelligently, and thus devotedly, the Gregorian which Vatican II has just reaffirmed as the supreme model of all sacred music, it should be the religious women who are allowed to stand in the sanctuary and give their lives exclusively to the things of the spirit.

It is often stated, with a sad wag of the head, that youth today is critical. Girls used to take things for granted. Now they have been educated to ask the reasons for things. Why should we fear their asking questions if we have the answers? Why should we fret at their wanting reasons if we know the reasons? And if we cannot answer the questions they raise and do not know the reasons why we live as we live and do as we do in the cloister, then the blame is with us, not with them. And the solution to the problem is not to reduce the modern girl to silence, but to enlarge ourselves to a better understanding of our vocation. We cannot do this by forever peering farsightedly at the past, though it is certainly true that we gather our strength from the past. Here again is where federations so wonderfully put the hyperopic god in his place, which is at the optometrist's.

There is no reason to swoon with dismay because postulants are critical when they enter. Give them answers. Provide them with reasons. If, after that, they persist in being critical, it is still not time to swoon with dismay, though it may well be time to dismiss the postulants. God can permit us to be questioned so as to remind us that we are expected to know answers.

The truest loyalty to a foundress of ancient times, the deepest fidelity to rule, is to the spirit expressed in the letter. We reverence the letter which defines the spirit. When the letter obviously no longer defines the spirit which is living and progressive, then, if it is a question of rule, we simply continue to reverence and learn from and nurture ourselves on the spirit while frankly admitting that the letter is no longer practicable. If it is a question of constitutions, we submit our case to the Church and ask that the letter be changed. St. Colette, less than two centuries after the death of St. Clare, was writing constitutions which flatly stated that points of the rule were no longer practicable and were even, in a few cases, now harmful. Colette was no devotee of the hyperopic god, any more than Clare, whom the popes of her time called "a new leader of women." If ever a woman was valiant in undertaking the new for valid reasons, it was St. Clare, who bypassed all traditional forms of religious life for women to establish a completely unique one.

The office of the hyperopic god is to sow bewilderment which makes it difficult to disentangle spirit from letter. "*Ipsi peribunt, tu autem permanes, et omnes sicut vestimentum veterascent. Et sicut opertorium mutabis eos et mutabuntur. Tu autem idem ipse es, et anni tui non deficient.*" (Ps. ci, 27-28)[1] We have only to substitute "spirit of the Order" for "*tu,*" and "letter of the law" for "*ipsi,*" and the whole point is made with perfect psalmodic conciseness. The hyperopic god is swung around by his ears and made to squint forward at the life-giving and energizing sun.

A veiled woman even outside a cloister in medieval times was nothing to make a passerby turn his head. A portress inside a cloister in modern times who appears with completely black-veiled face to tell the plumber what is wrong with the drain is an anachronism who achieves nothing except possibly to make the plumber cast uneasy glances at the exit.

---

[1] "They shall perish but thou remainest: and all of them shall grow old like a garment: and as a vesture thou shalt change them, and they shall be changed. But thou art always the selfsame: and thy years shall not fail."

St. Clare and St. Colette wanted the Poor Ladies to wear linen veils and guimpes. It would be no poor lady today who covered her head with black linen at $3.75 per yard. And so we change these things.

Many little fears arise from confusing renovation with innovation, minor panics at the idea of new horizons, acute pains in the region of the loyalty brought on by indigestion of adaptation. The fears need to be banished, the panic dissolved, the pains sedated. Yet, it is not a bad thing that they exist. It is, in fact, a very wonderful thing. What a frightening state that would be in which nuns gathered together, eyes bright with eagerness for changes and relaxations. What a dark assembly that would be of nuns rubbing their hands with expectation of shaking the dust of the past forever off their bare feet. It is certainly better that they meet instead with eyes bright with the old ideals, and conscious that ideals do not change but only the expression of them. It is their glory that they assemble with their hands clasping the rule book against their hearts.

> Come from the desert reaches
> And out of the metropolitan hearts of cities,
> Leave the long plains heaving spring
> Out of the winter-sleeping earth.
> Come on blue-veined feet,
> Come under cloistering veils,
> Swirl of long skirt for cadence on the hour,
> Sounding castanets of cross and bead,
> Arch of hand and pillaring fingers
> Sheltering breviary.

Bring your separate witness to the trial
Of unity made prosecute by separation,
And swear it, sing it,
Shout it with your silence:
How love is here enriched with love
And heart meets heart closer than touch of hand.

Across what miles, down into what abyss
Of strangeness, difference, fear, interpretation,
Love reaches, surer than logic,
Firmer than all convictions,
And flings us onto the breast
Of the Holy Spirit.

That is the way it appeared to one delegate at the federal chapter, and doubtless to them all.

Of all the strange gods who haunt cloisters, the hyperopic god is probably the most persistent. Nuns are equipped by their womanly nature to be tenacious of purpose and profoundly loyal to an ideal. They are further formed by their vocation to absolute fidelity. It only requires humility and patience to reject the heresy of the hyperopic god, the same remedies employed against the top-heavy god. Humility to admit the fatal weakness that can threaten our greatest strength; patience to disentangle the unchangeable from the healthily changing. It is because humility and patience are the particular tools of federations that the hyperopic god curses the day they were formed.

And so the best possible way to leave a federal chapter is the way the first capitulars left it, still clasping their rule books to their hearts, but as religious women better educated to appreciate that rule. It was as well a proof of the womanly triumph of the federation as of sisterly love, that the abbesses and delegates leaving Cleveland and the community remaining in Cleveland parted with tears sufficient to do credit to an Irish wake.

7

The Myopic God

The truckdriver was interested in that new rectangular building pinkly cheerful in the sunlight, topped with a large crucifix pure white against the clear blue April sky. He had driven into the enclosure with heavy sacks of chow too heavy for nuns to carry, for Lulu our cow. And though the portresses had never before extended monastic small talk beyond "Good morning!" when he came, and "Thank you, God bless you!" when he left, with perhaps a properly thoughtful "Yes, it is!" when he gave his opinion that it was a cold morning, he ventured farther today. He had to know.

This big sprawling building he did know. He was familiar with the old frame side and the new brick wing. He understood where the chapel and choir quarters jutted out with their bigger and more beautiful windows. But this little building was brand new. "What's that new little house?" he wanted to know, pointing a brown finger at the squat pinkish rectangle. Sister Paschal was busily locking the gate to Lulu's private grounds, so it was left to Sister Dolores to make the revelation. "That's our burial vault," she smilingly informed him.

We had been accustomed to a garden cemetery, but when our archbishop warned us that permission for this would probably not be given by the city officials, Mother Abbess began consulting other abbesses of monasteries having burial vaults instead of lawn cemeteries. She found to her glad surprise that, in the end, they proved cheaper. No graves to dig. Just open the door of a compartment and slide the departed Poor Clare in. No coffin, just a plain slab. All very simple. And *cheap*.

So the burial vault had been built, after long scraping of pennies, much hard work, and many raffles, including that of a Poor Clare doll who looked quite unconcerned about things eschatological. The regular routine for several Saturdays had been a rush for the uncompleted vault at the recreation following dinner dishwashing ceremonies. We climbed in and out of the upper compartments. The youngest nuns crawled in and out of the lowest openings. There was heated bidding for special places, and discussion about whether we were to be slid in feet first or head first, until Sister Beatrice learnedly pointed out that it should be head first, so that when the final trumpet sounded and the dead nuns all sat up, they would be facing the chapel.

At last the vault, if not the payment, was completed, the hinges set in place, the tiles of Our Lady of Guadalupe and St. Clare brought to us from Mexico by Archbishop Byrne erected, the ambulatory laid, the crucifix lifted up. And we loved it. Sundays and holidays, free moments between-times, would never fail to discover one or the other nun thoughtfully pacing the ambulatory or standing back for a long survey of her last resting place. Novices in summer retreat sat on pieces of stump by the bamboo tree (which Sister Assumpta persisted in watching for monkeys) and meditated on the escha-

tological significance of religious vows. Sister Juliana made a
shrine of St. Francis next to the vault, remembering his love
of Sister Death. And sometimes we had recreation in front of
the vault. Why not? It was already a familiar part of our home,
the monastic wing into which we would all eventually move.

This truckdriver, however, shared none of our enthusiasm
for death and burial vaults. "Burial vault?" he echoed, appearing to clear the ground by an inch or so. "Right there?
Right in your back yard?" Now Sister Dolores admires our
burial vault. Perhaps preoccupation with her admiration
made her somewhat obtuse. "Yes," she said proudly; "it's so
handy." Sister Paschal joined her at that moment, just in time
to see the American flag ripple, but not in the breeze. It was
the flag tatooed on the truckdriver's arm, rippling with his
alarm. "Anybody in there?" he asked in a hoarse whisper.
"No," replied Sister Dolores with the proper tone of apology
in her voice; "we usually live quite a long time." She added
more brightly: "But the Sisters love to meditate on death there.
The vault is such a nice reminder." The truckdriver leaped
into his cab. He leaned down. "You can never get out of here,
can you?" Sister Dolores smiled reproachfully. "We don't want
to get out." The truckdriver shot her and Sister Paschal an
appraising glance which said: "Well, it's all a matter of taste."
He stepped hard on the clutch, lowered his head slightly over
the wheel, and drove out through the enclosure gates. Fast.

The trouble with the truckdriver was that he had spiritual
myopia about death. Many of us have spiritual myopia about one
thing or another. And it is for that reason that some of us can
hack away rather too enthusiastically at ideas we have just never
got into proper focus because of mental nearsightedness. Thus,
inability to see the forest for the trees has been a recognized visual
liability through the ages. But it is a greater liability not to

understand that the trees constitute the forest. A tree is not a forest. Twelve trees do not qualify as a forest. Twenty-five trees might not be accepted as a forest. But a fine piece of research for a dedicated statistician would be to determine exactly what percentage of the trees in a forest could be cut down before we ceased to have a forest. His assistant might make experiments to indicate which particular tree's felling marked the end of the forest.

Sometimes people, and particularly nuns (who, despite some contrary opinion, are people and even persons), cannot see what is happening in the immediate vicinity because the hyperopic vision from which they suffer will not allow them to see well except at a distance. Some other times people, nuns among them, are so afflicted with myopic vision that they simply cannot get perspective on things. There is no possibility of their stepping back for a clear look at a thing in relation to other things. As soon as they do, the thing ceases properly to exist in their vision. This is what some of the too-ardent campaigners for wholesale adaptation of religious life do. They see this particular thing right in front of them, and it appears ridiculous. And so they wish to "adapt" it, by which they usually mean to abolish if not demolish it. All the time they have failed to see what this particular thing looks like in the broader setting which is its only proper setting.

This is the delight and the victory of the myopic god who insists that anything which is directly in front of his clients' eyes and does not justify itself as an immediate end must be swept away and abolished with enthusiastic cries about meeting the challenge of the times. This is scarcely what the popes of the last three decades have meant. This is hardly the mind of the Church, the Bride of Christ, who keeps her own twenty-

twenty vision trained compassionately on all her hyperopic and myopic children.

Each morning at Prime, Holy Church puts on the lips of her monks and nuns a paradoxical prayer. It is a plea that we may be ruled and governed by the Lord. It continues, very specifically, that our thoughts, our words, our actions be subject to Him, directed toward Him. The paradox lies in what might seem an astonishing conclusion: "in order that we may be worthy to be free." There it is. The *bon mot*, the pennant of the modern crusaders, the call to arms against invasion by authority. Freedom! Liberation!

Certainly the Church is all for it. It is only her means to the end that nettle the extremists. This business of subjection, dependence, submission has a dangerous ring. It sounds like that worst of bogeys, traditionalism, to those who feel it is time that Holy Church, along with her contemplatives, got a hustle on. Although no one would suggest that the prayer be changed to run like this: "That deciding for ourselves what we shall do or shall not do, and discarding all old ways because they are old, we shall demonstrate our newness, bring our personalities to luxuriant bloom, and be free," still the avant garde does demand: "Let us be free!" Many a contemplative nun adds to that supplication a smiling: "God save us!" remembering that we must first be worthy to be free.

Freedom is assuredly dear to God. We know this because He made us so free, leaves us so free, that we can even go right ahead and damn ourselves to an eternity of hell with no ultimate pressure from Him. His love will invite us to be bound to Him. His grace will suggest the glory of dependence on infinite power. But an omnipotent God will never force His small human creatures. We are indeed supremely free in this greatest possible sense of the word. The only trouble about damnation freely chosen is that it lands us in a state of no choice. Hell, once won, has no electives. We can be glib with phrases like "glorious freedom!" Perhaps we do not often enough ponder how terrible and even terrifying our freedom is, heaven or hell within our choosing.

In the matter of adaptation of religious life, we are not, of course, driven to heaven-or-hell decisions. We are concerned only with finding a better or a best means to a particular end. Still, it is not out of place to do a little reflecting about the limits of freedom, even for good people engaged in rethinking good things with the hope of making them better.

Freedom is formally, and poorly enough, defined as liberation from slavery, imprisonment, restraint. It is usually the last that is seized upon with burning zeal by those whose concept of freedom may seem quite profound until we chip at its varnish and discover the flaws and the hollowness beneath. This is not at all to say that most of the pleaders for innovation in religious life are not wise and holy. The whole thing reduces to a matter of perspectives, false and true.

Why are certain persons delivering spirited talks on the need for greater and greater adaptation in female religious life, and many female religious getting wearier and wearier? Adaptation is such a very good thing. The popes urge it. Intelligent religious know that it is essential if their Orders are not to gasp their last and become mere historical memories. The trouble is the false perspective of the myopic. The bad thing is extremism. We need to recall to ourselves now and again that if everything old is not good, still everything old is not bad; and that everything new is not good, even though many new things are very good indeed. Extremism in certain quarters has brought a good thing, adaptation, to that painful stage of discussion where many a nun listens with reactions comparable to those of a hay fever victim who fell into a barrel of pollen.

Contemplative Orders would seem to be the ones best qualified to present the case against extremism in adaptation. The
Poor Clares, for example, have been tottering along traditional paths for longer than seven hundred and fifty years
now. By all odds, the creatures should have been extinct by at
least 1920, the first era of visible knees. But there they are,
still locked up in their cloisters, still barefoot, still fasting and
abstaining from meat around the clock and around the year,
still enjoying the pleasure of going to bed twice every night
because they still get up twice, still practising corporal penances and submitting themselves to a tight minutiae. And,
worst of all, appearing to like this sort of thing.

The case should be clear. Surely they must be on the way
out of the modern world, the "modern Church"? It is downright embarassing for the extremist crusaders to stub their toes
on the hard facts, which are: in the last ten years, there has
been a marked increase of contemplative vocations in this
country. In the last six or seven years, the increase has been
notable among the Poor Clares. More distressing still is the
fact that the vocations tilting the number upward are not dull-
eyed girls unorientated toward any kind of fresh thinking,
unable to make their way in a forward-looking world. No,
they come from the college classroom, the art studio and
drama department, the literary seminar, the streamlined office,
and other supposed strongholds of free thought and personality
development. It is the lively, successful, capable girls who are
tilting the number upward.

When the myopic god casts his very limited glance around
a Poor Clare cloister in Lent, he sees things that offend his
sensibilities, wring his progressive heart, and revolt his crusad-
ing spirit. Why do the nuns stand up to eat their small break-

fast? No Lenten fast requires this. And if they must stand, can't they stand there like sensible people, decently shod instead of barefoot? Who ever said you couldn't love God with your shoes on? Why, on Fridays, do they cast down their veils on the floor and stretch out their arms to pray the psalm *"Miserere mei"*? Why does an older nun kneel down before young nuns and even before novices and postulants, and humbly beg each one to pray that she may become a good religious? This is surely theatrical. And, even outside Lent and thus even less excusably, why should a grown woman be expected to do down on both knees in the refectory just because her sleeve swiped against her knife and fork and swept them onto the floor with a resounding crash? Heavens, it was only an accident. Nothing malicious about it.

Then there is the major point of the myopic god about all these and a hundred other similar monastic usages: they are not essential to religious life. They can be updated or, much better, uprooted without affecting what is fundamental to religious life in the least. Likewise, we can pray sitting down if we do not feel like kneeling. We can love God in the coolest possible garments in summer and the very warmest in winter. We can multiply gadgets and worldly conveniences in the name of saving time, even though we may not be very clear about what we are saving it for. In other words, we can know God, love God, and serve God as comfortably as possible.

This is where we shall need that statistician, however, to inform us at which particular tree we must halt our felling enterprise lest we cease to have a forest any longer, where to stop keeping up with the times lest we become the sorriest product of our times: religious hurrying to adapt what they have not stopped long enough to understand. We must first know what our goal is and where it lies before we give our full attention to changing the means of locomotion. We need to take care that in an excess of enthusiasm we do not adapt our life right out of existence.

The myopic god is twin to the surface god, but not an identical twin. Where the surface god sternly forbids his devotees to seek the fruit beneath the skin, the myopic god will not even admit that skin is skin, fulfilling its office of preserving the fruit and, in some cases, holding the fruit together as a unit. He is too nearsighted to make any valid conclusions about either skin or fruit. And he should not, therefore, demand that we toss all fruit into the garbage can because he happened to eat a few worms he had not seen.

Each vocation in life has its specific genius. What is proper to one cannot be wholly proper to another. A married woman, a nurse, a nun should each dress according to her station, spiritually, mentally, materially. The stations are not the same. The dedicated teaching sister and the dedicated contemplative nun are dedicated in the same love to the same God and the same souls, but the means and thus the appurtenances of the dedication are quite different. Some of the excesses in over-urging adaptation and updating arise from a failure to comprehend that the service of God is diversely rendered, and the love of God and souls demonstrated in many different although equally valid ways.

Over-zealous myopics must gently be made aware of this myopia. The people of God form one family, but each one in the family has his own face and fingerprints; and each cell its own proper sphere and even its own proper uniform. If only the myopic god could get a good visual correction so that he could step back and enjoy a better and fuller look at life, many things would appear as what they truly are: different means to a single end. And they would show themselves to be means with great meaning. They would make wonderfully good sense. In a cloister he would then be able to get a better line on certain usages which, taken individually, could nettle, but when taken as a whole not only justify their existence but define the vocation to which they very validly belong.

Pope Pius XII wrote emphatically in his apostolic constitution, *Sponsa Christi*, of the *"rigida et dura disciplina"* of a nun's life, stating in paragraph three, article two, that, in the case where contemplative life under this *"rigida regularis disciplina"* cannot be habitually followed out by a community, such a community must renounce the monastic character and pass into the category of Sisters. It is this "strict and austere discipline," says the pope, which is the indispensable condition of the nun's life. There is nothing wrong with being comfortable, of course, except that a girl does not enter a cloister to be comfortable. The particular kind of service God asks of her, the vocation which is the answer to her desire, is precisely a *"rigida et dura disciplina."* She has come for it. It would be unfair to her not to let her find it, since it is only under a *"rigida disciplina"* that she will be able to taste the sweet freedom of service in which there is no rigidity. It is one of the oldest paradoxes of monastic life that one arrives at freedom precisely and solely by way of a strict discipline of life. It all refers back to that prayer at Prime: that being ruled and governed by Him we may be worthy to be free.

In all adaptation, we cannot make even an intelligent beginning without informing ourselves first of the paritcular end for which a society was established. We need to be sure what its particular apostolate is before we can speak competently about how it can best fulfill its apostolate. There are, for instance, external alleviations as well as adaptations which are entirely proper to Sisters carrying an extremely heavy teaching load, to religious nurses whose dedication exacts a physical and emotional toll which calls for physical and psychological refuellings, but which would not be proper to contemplatives whose apostolate does not lie in the classroom or in the ward but directly in the spirit. That active Sisters, at least as far as our experience extends, humbly respect the austerities proper to cloistered nuns, while the latter are filled with humble admiration for the sacrificial work of their active Sisters, is normal and natural. Each has her own form of holocaust reverenced by the other. Each group has a common end reached by a different means, each aware that the circumstances as well as the manner of the holocaust will and should inevitably differ.

Once we briefly had a very forthright postulant. When, after a one-week sojourn in the monastery, she decided the life was not for her, Sandra had a candid and comprehensive reply for the mistress who inquired as to what had led to her quick decision to leave. Said Sandra on that August day: "You work too hard. You pray too much. And it's hot." Outside of that, no doubt, she found everything idyllic. But Sandra contributed nothing to the folio on adaptation except the fact that she did not have a vocation. To the girl with a vocation to the cloistered life of prayer and penance, as much as to the girl with a vocation to the married life, it is always a question of the maximum one can give in that particular kind of vocation, not the minimum.

Pope Pius XII also pointed out that, "This apostolate which the Church entrusts to nuns is performed by them in three ways: by the example of Christian perfection which silently draws the faithful to Christ; by public and private prayer; by the zeal to practise, besides the penitence prescribed by the Rule, all that is suggested by the generous love of the Lord."[1]

[1] Three Radio Addresses of Pope Pius XII to Contemplative Nuns Throughout the World, August 2, 1958; Chinigo, *op. cit.*

And the very forthright postulants who come and who do not go are precisely those who wish not just to work, but to work hard, not only to pray, but to pray always, and who keep their vision clear in haze of heat and thrust of cold. They are the educables who can appreciate the difficult immediate as part of a magnificent ultimate and a really glorious whole.

It would be interesting to know where certain current writers, notably all male, get their statistics for statements so sweeping as to leave nun readers sneezing from the dust. After we have been informed that the chapter of faults accomplishes no good, the discipline is obsolete, community recreation a bore, and community life in general just material for the gnashing of teeth, we are assured that customs are mainly nuisances and regulations only restrictions, and finally warned that superiors are commonly jealous authoritarians who get jaundice when a subject has an idea of her own. The modern Poor Clare novice lately come from the Blackfriars' stage or Missouri University or the offices of United Steel can reply in language quite as crisp as that of the masculine excoriator when she counters: "Who says?" (Poor Clare novices are obviously the only ones about whom a competent opinion can be given here, but certainly the same would be true of intelligent novices in any cloister, anywhere.)

It is such a foolish, and even a tragic, blunder to expect too little of youth. It may be true that girls who enter religion today have, in some sense at least, more to "give up" than girls of earlier generations. Youth today is generally better educated to independent thinking and also more besieged by materialistic values than youth of fifty years ago. Basically, however, a girl breaks with the same ties that the postulant of 1900 broke with, and for the same reason. Love is still what brings girls into cloisters and keeps them there. Love is still what transcends pleasure. And love is still the only right impulse toward penance, without which it is quite meaningless. Still, when we consider the more liberal allowances, the private cars, the position in the business world, or the social and cultural opportunities a modern postulant has had, we realize that she has had certain allurements to cast off that her predecessors in the cloister had not. The trouble is that certain current writers and counsellors advise that because a girl has sacrificed a great deal to enter religious life, it is the bounden duty of superiors to make religious life easier for her. This is a very strange conclusion. Because a girl has been willing to give up much to enter a cloister, we must see to it that she need give little in the cloister? This is the kind of reasoning in which the myopic god excels since he is unable to envision things in proper focus or proportion.

If we "tone down" the sacrifices, streamline the work, soften the penance, and take the big, broad view of things like silence and recollection, self-abasement and self-denial, we are doing a supreme injustice to a girl who elected to forego worldly pleasure and possible worldly acclaim in favor of a *"rigida et dura disciplina"* in the cloister. We also do a double injustice to the community, for by planing down the cross, we encourage the mediocre or even those plainly lacking a vocation to remain, and the best subjects to go. For the girl of high ideals who cannot find the means to realize them in the cloister will certainly go, one way or another. That is, she will go out of the monastery and back into the world, or she will go out of her high aspirations and live an increasingly unhappy life of compromises.

It is possible that we might have adapted our way of life to suit Sandra's ideas, shortened the work schedule, reduced the prayer time, and installed air conditioning. Sandra might still be with us. Very likely, Linda, Therese, and Pauline, even newly-come Carole, would not. The girl with the true vocation wants to serve God the hard way, by which is meant in the fullest possible way. For her, it is the easier way because it is the only way. The community has a duty to provide and a right to expect the sacrificial life which a postulant comes desirous to live.

Perhaps it would be well to recall here that we are not speaking of the adaptation proper to all religious in a changing world, which is very good, but of the extremist views of myopic adaptation, which are very bad.

April is always April each new year, no matter how many years have been eternally calendared. Youth is always enthusiastic, idealistic, capable of conceiving and executing great and noble works. We betray our April-aged religious when we water down the monastic ideal. We ought rather to challenge today's postulants to the heights of self-immolation and the most searching kind of holocaust, remembering that the girl who "gave up" most gave it up because she wanted to give even more. The myopic god is too nearsighted to get the full picture from back or front. He urges excessive and false adaptation upon his myopic subjects because for him there are no ultimates, no comprehensive views. He sees not a life of penance, but one penance at a time, which cannot, of course, make any particular or compelling sense of its own.

Beautifully, Lent is usually boundaried with April. The most exquisite month of the year is marked off by Lenten austerities. Is there not great significance in this? Myrrh is a preservative. It is the *"rigida et dura disciplina"* which keeps monastic life forever young, fresh, and vigorous. And it is a comfortable, cozy monastic life which is old, stale, and manifestly senile in trying to abolish that which is its strength, seeking to abrogate its birthright.

Neither long skirts, bare feet, chapter of faults, dry bread, or penances for faults are ends in themselves. But how can the myopics understand this? They cannot see, except up close and one thing at a time. Sometimes a layman will show more spiritual insight into nuns' practices of penance and humility than certain clerical writers, and be less than agitated by monastic customs that reduce certain militant activists to groans. When our postulant Therese had only recently entered the cloister and had enthusiastically written to her parents about some of the penitential practices, including the supposed bogey of kneeling down to touch one's lips to the floor if one made a loud noise or disturbance at table, her father, who probably kept fresh green memories of Therese's noisy domestic manoeuvres, wrote back serenely: "Well, honey, you must be on the floor a good part of the time."

To cling to theatrical medieval practices of penance just because they were performed in the past is patently foolish. However, it is just as foolish to abandon fruitful practices of penance simply because they belong to the past. The present moves forward in exactly the measure in which it gathers wisdom from the past. If ancient usages continue to be conducive to humility, charity, and patience, then they are as modern as they are ancient. If they are not, then it is time to think about updating or maybe even abolishing them. But we shall first want to make sure that something is really wrong with the usage and not instead something wrong with the nun.

If girls who have only just doffed their white high-school or black college mortarboards, who have very recently put off their nurses' caps or set down their secretarial notebooks, come into a cloister and are easily able to grasp, on the Fridays of an April Lent, why the nuns cast down their veils, the symbols of their dignity, when they stretch out their arms in supplication for sinners, there would seem to be no particular need to adapt what is intrinsically adaptable, that is, ageless. From another perspective, it is more than dubious that postulants who cannot be educated to understand that performing a little act of penance for making a loud noise is a thing intimately connected with a sense of one's unworthiness to be a member of God's household, and with that refinement of humility which fears ever to intrude on the recollection of the companions one regards as superior to oneself, will ever understand much of anything else about cloistered religious life, either. The young must learn from the old in religion, but the old always learn from the young as well. And it is educational for the old, as well as distinctly comforting, to hear a young postulant's sage appraisal of an ancient way of life: "It is so—right."

As with religious usages, so with that tender subject, religious garb. If nuns wrote half as many discourses on the vagaries of lay*women's* fashions as lay*men* do on those of religious, the world's ink supply would sink to a dangerously low level. Pope Pius XII urged adaptation in religious dress where it was needed, and very many Orders and Congregations have followed his suggestion, not, it is true, at anything like a whirlwind pace, but more at the wise pace at which he himself first proposed, then permitted, and only later enforced the ancient order of Holy Week and the Easter Vigil. It is more than doubtful that saintly Pius expected all religious women, the day after his first injunction, to raise their hems and undo their coifs.

Adaptation of religious dress does not mean that there must remain no discernible difference between the airline hostess and the nun. Nor does it mean that every existing religious habit is, ipso facto, hopeless. It is doubtful whether any man fully understands what her religious dress, veiled head, and cincture mean to a religious woman, yet certain male writers seem to feel a driving sense of obligation to tell the religious woman that it does not mean anything, really. Many a layman apparently does not stop to cap his fountain pen after writing out the $25.oo check for his wife's newest horror-hat before he begins an impassioned essay on the need for nuns to discard their coifs.

Hats have always fascinated me, as they do most women. I remember venturing, when I was sixteen, into a very exclusive hat salon in company with my friend, Florence. We probably did not have between us the price of one hat on display, but the trying-on process was great fun. I recall a bright rust-colored, three-tiered bonnet with a veil that fell over my face and below my shoulders, and which I felt with a delicious thrill made me look like the most bored of all bored sophisticates. The salesgirl seemed enchanted with me in the hat, too. She stepped back, drew a deep breath, and half closed her eyes as she indicated inspiration by an upraised, scarlet-nailed finger. "My dear!" She closed her eyes all the way and bit delicately at her underlip. "It's for *you!*"

What we wear in the cloister is neither stylish nor unstylish, but a-stylish. It's "for us." When we found that the wimple needed simplifying, we simplified it. There is no reason to suppose any other religious are less well-intentioned or intelligent. And if some have thought they had no need to change where onlookers felt a change was indicated, who is to judge that this is "stubbornness"? Again, it is the very writers who belabor religious superiors for not giving sufficient quarter to the opinions and judgments of their subjects who also belabor religious superiors for not riding roughshod over the opinions of their subjects in this matter of dress.

The mute reminder of God and spiritual values which a religious habit always is will not be happily removed from our boulevards and airlines. Certain male writers insist on the advantages of religious wearing ordinary street dress when not in their convents, although they invariably fail to mention what these advantages are. Some modern social congregations do this to good purpose because it is part of the genius of their organizations, but it would be rash and quite unreal to urge this on religious whose congregations or orders have an entirely different genius. Besides the universal respect for the religious garb which immediately sets the woman consecrated to God apart (and that this respect extends even to pagans, drunks, and assorted cads is well known), there are profound reasons for the continual wearing of a particularized religious garb which cannot be disposed of with a facile and undocumented "advantageous." As a matter of fact, the religious habit is least needed within the convent where spiritual values are already the only values by which the inmates try to live.

Then, again, what *is* "ordinary street dress"? A cloistered nun will not be involved in this proposal unless it is intended that she, too, wear a blouse and skirt when she has to go to the hospital, but when on such an occasion she sees the narrow, shapeless shifts women are wearing today, she is apt to wonder if by any chance they forgot to finish dressing and came out in their slips. But then, in a few years, this will no longer be ordinary street dress, either. What will be?

Religious dress is also part of a larger picture which the myopic god is not equipped to see, so large as to cross over into the boundaries of eternal values. Books written at 240-blood pressure throughout fail to take this into account. If we step back from what directly confronts our gaze, we shall see things more as a whole and be able to talk of adaptation calmly and intelligently as, thank God, most people do. It is only that the 240-blood pressures are such Passionately Dedicated Men that extremism appears to hold a prominence it does not actually have at all.

In April when the burial vault here is so freshly outlined against a blue curve of sky, Carole and Therese go out to plant bright marigolds and delicate larkspur around it. They love the vault. We love the vault. We step back from it and see it for what it is: a literal low gateway leading into life. If it did not lead anywhere, it might appear as gruesome a reminder to us as it did to the truckdriver. Like him, we might want to adapt it out of our back yard. Because, instead, it is a symbol of final freedom, the freedom of which we are trying to become worthy in the manner indicated by the second prayer at Prime, we reverence it. Just so do we reverence the garb which is a symbol of a woman's love freely given and part of a large idea of consecration. Just so do we reverence the penances which are expressions of dedication as also of hope, and part of a large idea of reparation.

Francis Thompson showed himself no worshipper of the myopic god when he wrote:

> Hardest servitude has he
> That's jailed in arrogant liberty;
> And freedom, spacious and unflawed
> Who is walled about with God.

8

The Neurotic God in His Study

Pauline looks the incarnation of a morning in May on this May morning of her investiture as a novice. As she stands in a billow of ivory shantung with her sunlight-gold hair falling down to her shoulders, she is quite the twentieth-century American counterpart of young Clare of Assisi, even to the color of her hair. Small, excited sparrows are hurrying about Our Lady's patio just outside the choir, and Sister Celine reported yesterday that the swallows have returned and are building an apartment under the roof of the front porch. Linda, Therese, and Carole have picked little green peas from the garden for Pauline's investiture dinner. Tall scented irises border the lawns, flank the burial vault, and line the driveway, an honor guard in white and yellow, rust and lavender for God's young fiancée. The freshness and tenderness of May lies like a sweet-smelling mantle over the monastery, and everyone shares with Pauline the sense of a new beginning. Another contemplative May bud is at the threshold of its flowering.

But why does the spiritual bud which is the soul of a young religious sometimes never open into the promised flower?

Why do some fail to achieve either their private destiny of spiritual fulfilment or the fullness of their role in the community? There are perhaps more reasons than this brief consideration could hope to cover, but certainly one very prominent and painfully common reason is that worst kind of neuroticism which is the unrecognized neuroticism. It is not a case of any virulent form of abstraction from reality. Would that it were! Heavy dosing and therapy can do something for the virus. It is the "mild attack," the light chronic form of withdrawal from reality, which is most elusive of cure simply because it is so respectable and so persistent.

A young novice is determined to give herself entirely to God. Yet sometimes she has neither become well aquainted with herself nor even been properly introduced to herself by those who should help and guide her. She wants to give, but has only a vague and confused notion of what it is she has to give. And so she charts her new life by a pole-star which is, for her, nothing but an illusion. She begins chasing the phantoms of that dubious spirituality which assures her that all she has to do is uproot one fault after another, according to number and kind, and then present herself a pure and spotless gift to God. Six months to pull up impatience, one year to obliterate a really stubborn pride, three months to fumigate vanity, and,—presto!—perfection!

She becomes fired with the desire to put off the old man, but in a way Christ never intended. What she aspires to do is to tear down the nature God gave her and become the great saint He never meant her to be—that is, St. Somebody Else instead of St. Myself. And the neurotic god has good cause to rub his hands together expectantly. He may be about to annex another chronic client or, more precisely, to victimize another young religious.

It is strange what outrageous things we will easily believe of God. Even in elementary school we heard Father declare at the eight o'clock children's Mass that Christ loves each and every one of us with an individual love so great and so unique that He would have died on the Cross for a single one of us. Yet, in adult life, our striving for perfection can sometimes reduce itself to an effort to become not the perfected individual God uniquely created, but a featureless neuter compound of "perfection."

We admit that God gave us a very specific human nature, a distinct personality, a particular combination of qualities; and then we persuade ourselves that He wants us to raze this nature and build another of our own making, unravel this personality and weave a new one, scramble this combination of qualities and set up an entirely different ratio. God has never asked the impossible of anyone. And although His cool injunction to "be perfect as your heavenly Father is perfect" might appear impossible, we know it is not, or He could not have asked it. There is no inconsistency in God, although there is considerable inconsistency in us. If He holds up nothing less than divine perfection as a human ideal, He must have provided divine means to attain the ideal. He did, of course. It is grace.

On the other hand, God would not be God if He required Sister Dolores to be perfect as Sister Paschal is perfect. This would indeed have been to ask the impossible. He does not want Sister Juliana to become St. Celine, but St. Juliana. Nor has He required a woman to love Him with a man's nature, but with her own. And in the mixture of light and shade which the Divine Omniscience mingled in mysterious proportions in each individual one of us, He never suggested that we take an axe to every shade tree in us, but only that the light should gradually dissipate the shade. As the light of grace moves to its zenith, which is death, its triumph will be to shine upon the tall trees within us, not to discover them neatly uprooted and dead upon the ground.

We are facile enough with the phrase that "grace builds on nature," but sometimes very slow and stupid about trying to build along with grace instead of against it. When we speak of faults which must be uprooted, unfortunately we often really mean tendencies which must be destroyed. Yet God gave us our particular tendencies for good. When they take the direction of evil, His grace is there to help us redirect them, not to stomp them out of existence.

How many frustrations, black depressions, bitter disappointments in the spiritual life are traceable to the misspent energy of working against the very things we should be working to perfect. In every virtue there is a seed of vice. We are a fallen race. Yet every vice is, in the deepest sense, only a virtue run wild, run in fact to ruin.

That glorious company of the saints is comprised of numberless copies of Christ. But no two copies look alike. Each saint once had to love God and serve Him with a highly distinct and individual combination of qualities, insights, capabilities. And not one of them ever took this human nature by the throat and strangled it. Nor did he take his personality by the shoulders to shake the very life out of it. No, he built sanctity under the direction of grace on the only nature he had to build on. He accepted his God-given personality and developed it in faith and in love. In faith, because it can often require a great faith to believe it is possible to become perfect as the heavenly Father is perfect while carrying the particular crushing load which is myself. In love, because it is only love which ever accomplishes anything of lasting worth.

While the neurotic god is presenting to his prospective converts his doctrine of destruction speciously entitled "perfection," the saints of God are shouting out of heaven: Build!
build! Their glory is to have become eternally famous for the
very virtues to which their nature *seemed* most disinclined.
This is readily evident in many of them, and true of all of
them.

Francis of Assisi burned with ambition when he was a lovable
young roisterer in thirteenth-century Assisi. He wanted to excel.
By nature, he was then patently excelling in being a frivolous
spendthrift, already ambitious to be the best-armored, most victorious, most gallant of knights, winning at the end the fairest
lady of them all. When the grace of his vocation was given to
him by God, Francis did not begin (nor did he end) by laying
an axe to the roots of his nature. Because he had always been an
ambitious young man, he now became studiously ambitious to
be first in lowliness, first in humility, first in poverty. People
were soon shaking their heads anew over this young fellow.
They had sighed before at his excesses. They sighed now at his
excesses, only now it was a matter of excessive humility, excessive poverty, and excessive love of souls, where before it
had been an affair of excessive vanity, excessive spending, and
excessive affection for the supposed good things of this world.

Francis had always wanted to serve his king. He was by
nature a minstrel and a chivalrous knight. When he set about
becoming St. Francis or, to use an apter expression, set about
loving God with the undivided heart of a saint, he was very
consciously still in the service of a king—*the* King. He had
been endowed by God with a singing heart. If he sang once
for the very love of life, he sang all the more loudly and
engagingly now for the love of God. "I am the herald of the
great King," declared patched and barefoot Francis. He never

said a truer word. He did not found a conventional Order because he did not have a conventional nature. He gathered about him a group of happy nomads because he had a gypsy's heart and understood that it was his vocation and the vocation of his Order to remind men that the earth is not their home. And he never showed himself more ambitious than when he named his sons "the friars minor." He was ambitious that his followers, along with himself, should be not just humble, but the humblest of all, indicating by their very title that they were beneath all others in the Church. "Let us be tiny poor people," said Francis, who had once yearned for greatness and shown a particular talent for wasting money. This strange invitation was accepted by hundreds and then thousands of other men equally ambitious. Only those who lacked the capacity for such excessive ambition fell away from him and his ideals.

If Francis had worked against grace instead of with grace, if he had been horrified at the ambition and vanity he knew was in him, packed a bag and gone off to the desert to sweat the human nature out of himself, we would live today in a much poorer world. For we would not have the heritage of St. Francis who so redirected the tendencies of his own nature that he could cry out on his knees in a prison cell in Perugia one of the most magnificently humble avowals of sublime simplicity that the world has heard: "The whole world will run after me!"

Humility and poverty have become part of the very name of Francis, who was so inclined to be vain and spendthrift. "Il Poverello" is both his title and his triumph. "Humble St. Francis" is not an instance of an adjective modifier with a noun; it is one proper name. It might appear superficially that he became the opposite of himself. Actually, he built with grace upon the only self he had. And his humility is only the perfection of his ambition.

And then there was Clare. After she left her castle home and discovered for herself what servantless housekeeping was like in a dilapidated old monastery, she did not emerge as a "new woman" in the sense that she had destroyed the nature and personality of the gay, cherished, courted girl she had been, but as a newly grace-perfected version of herself. And so she wrote of the poverty which made her and her daughters "heiresses and queens," not of a poverty which made them austere wimpled spinsters. She had been a wealthy heiress. Hers was the nature of a queen. She simply let God perfect the nature He had given her. All her gracious life, even to its lovely exit line: "Be praised, my Lord, for having created me," she remained the aristocrat she had been born. Poverty and austerity did not coarsen her, they refined her the more; because for her, poverty and austerity were loved tools in the hands of grace, modelling and perfecting rather than destroying the material which was her self. If she had put on boots and armor instead of donning a habit and doffing her shoes, we would have neither two saints Joan nor one saint Clare. The two must be real friends in heaven. But they are not each other.

If we see this clearly enough, why can we not see with equal clarity that the hypersensitiveness which makes a nun an unpleasant cactus in the monastic plot is merely a God-given delicacy which took a wrong turn and must be gently led back by grace? The nun who thinks she is combatting her oversensitiveness by trying to render herself impervious to attack is wasting her time as well as God's grace. If she has this kind of nature, she will never succeed in not reacting to the merest slight or misunderstanding. She will not miss a nuance, ever, or be unaware of a gathering atmosphere. She is simply not emotionally fashioned to be a sack of potatoes and cannot become one. If she keeps striving to do so, she is instead likely to become a victim of the neurotic god. A nun who stops "overcoming" her sensitiveness in the sense of establishing an elaborate inner pretense that her nature does not quiver under the least misunderstanding, and loading herself with reproaches that it ought not, and instead works at redirecting her sensitiveness so that she acquires an extreme delicacy for the feelings of others, is a builder in the spiritual life and not a wrecker. Consequently, for all her faults and failures, she is a balanced personality who lives happily and constructively and creates happiness around her.

The quick-tempered and impatient nun who keeps trying to force a lid down on her nature all day long is less apt to end in equanimity than in explosion. For her to concentrate on being first to arrive at the work, first in eagerness to carry the heaviest part of the load, first in ingenuity to find ways to help the slow or the dull is to redirect the wonderful energies God put into her. Such a religious, instead of being the recognized community volcano to be skirted cautiously for fear of being struck by erupting lava, may come in God's slow time to be known as the most generous nun in the community.

God's slow time. Yes, because that is the only kind He seems to have. He waits for us, as we so often refuse to wait for Him. Waiting is at once the sternest and gentlest of arts. It cannot be taught and yet it must be learned. No one, however, is asked by God to become so practised and proficient in this art as the contemplative. May must slowly ripen into June, not erupt into it. And slowly, slowly will grace pumice the stone of human nature into its perfection of beauty. Axe blows destroy quickly, but pumicing slowly and painstakingly rubs off excrescences. In the name of striving for perfection, how often a religious will persistently withdraw from the reality which is herself. Unconsciouly, she is reproaching God for His creation and implying that He made a great error which her zeal must correct. Her tragic end is often a neurotic absorption with the false self she is trying to create, living in the haunted house of pretenses.

None of this is to suggest that making peace with one's faults is a praiseworthy thing, of course. As a matter of fact, that would be a most precarious peace and could only end in defeat not of the faults but of oneself, since making peace with one's faults actually means surrendering the victory to them. The person who snaps impatiently at anyone who does not match his own pace or agree with his own ideas, and who attempts to excuse his unlovely behavior with a definitive: "Well, that's the way I am; I can't help it," is merely saying that he is quite satisfied to be the way he is. The hypersensitive nun who sniffles or pouts her way through life and whispers through her damp handkerchief: "I can't help it that I feel things so deeply," is very likely not only at peace with her faults but rather proud of them. This is to be in an even worse state than that of the religious who is so determined to uproot her faults that she has dedicated her energies to uprooting her whole nature and so becomes the chronic neurotic.

It is the rechannelling and redirecting of good energies run amuck which makes the obligation of striving for perfection a glorious obligation and a constructive striving, despite the thousand failures. The saints were builders on the bedrock of the natures God gave them. Unhappy, frustrated, neurotic religious are often those who are working the hardest, but at wrecking not at constructing. Because they can never attain their goal and become people they are not, they must take one of two ways out of the neurotic labyrinth they have laid out in their own interiors, decide on one of two methods to get clear of the chaos they have created within themselves. One is to retreat into the neurotic dream world of a sustained pretense: I refuse to believe that I am myself, and I shall prove by my conduct that I am someone else. The second way is to admit that I cannot cope with myself, run up the white flag, and settle down into that most unrewarding kind of life which is mediocrity.

Yet, this type of person, in whichever of the two ways she decides to fail herself, her vocation, and her community, is still more aware of her obligation and more concerned with perfection (that is, with loving God in full measure) than the religious who makes her community an unhappier place because she is in it, with her ultimatum of: "That's the way I am." She is telling the community, as regards her nature and personality, to "take it or leave it." The community would doubtless prefer to leave it, but it scarcely can, especially if it is a cloistered community. Pressed far enough, this supine argument leads to the picture of the angry man with the smoking revolver, standing above the dead victim who annoyed him, and saying while he puts the gun away: "I couldn't help it. That's the way I am." The religious "at peace" with her impatience is a volcano in the community because she has failed to direct the immense God-given energies within her down the right paths of generosity and service. The hypersensitive nun "at peace" with her sensitiveness may become the cruellest nun in the community because she has turned her divine heritage of delicacy in upon herself instead of out upon others. Both are also species of the neurotic, unable or unwilling to face reality.

It is in our very faults that we must find by God's grace the radix of virtue. Just so, a nun must find the material for being a worthy nun in the exercise of her womanhood, not in the suppression of it. It is true that St. Teresa of Avila declared that she wanted her spiritual daughters to be manly, but this has to be read in context. Obviously, the saint was expressing her disgust with the sentimentality and pettiness which are the defects of womanliness, and went to a not too happy excess of word to make herself clear. The fact that the term "a manly woman" is often given as a tribute or accepted as a compliment, whereas the expression "a womanly man" would be considered an insult, only proves that womanhood has often not been properly evaluated or understood. The perfection of womanhood is womanliness, not manliness. St. Clare loved St. Francis with a surpassing love and called him "after God, our only pillar and support." But she became a saint and a perfect lover of God by perfecting the womanhood of Clare, not by trying to assume the manhood of Francis. The nun who is afraid of her womanhood, embarrassed by her womanhood, or worst of all, the enemy of her womanhood, is just another victim of the neurotic god.

The most un-nunly thing a nun can do is to forget, scorn or suppress her womanhood. Yet to attempt one or the other of these things is sometimes thought to be a worthy goal for a religious, and particularly for a cloistered religious. Her withdrawal from the world, her holocaust of self, is rightly expected to be as complete as is within human power inspired by God and aided by grace. It is sometimes wrongly expected, however, that this withdrawal and this holocaust are both accomplished and demonstrated by a coldness of manner and a flintiness of heart. These are not qualities characteristic of a normal woman. They need effort to acquire. And how much effort is wasted in pursuing these phantom goals, in desperately trying to acquire the very qualities which will prohibit a nun's ever realizing her nunliness which is only her innate womanliness released on a higher plane of consecrated virginity.

Without realizing what she is doing, a nun can work assiduously against all within her that would most glorify God. God made a woman to love and to be loved. He fashioned her tenderly and graciously. He gave her a rich, warm nature and a capacity for suffering quite peculiar to herself. She is not only physically equipped for childbearing, but mentally and emotionally planned by God for it. The fact that God sets aside some of these creatures so fashioned to be virginally His alters nothing of these qualities, destroys none of this equipment. To be a nun does not and must not mean to pass over into neuter gender. Quite the contrary. It means to be completely feminine, entirely a woman. It means, in fact, that one is expected by God to be more completely a woman. Yet it is a sad fact that many nuns are afraid to be women. And so they take their womanly nature by its throat, and place firm "virtuous" thumbs to press the life breath out of it. Apparently some succeed.

The very raison d'être of womanhood is love. The wife of a man and mother of his children is the better wife and mother the more she loves her husband and her children. The spouse of God most truly a spouse is the nun who loves Him and His vast progeny of souls with the full, rich love of her womanly heart. And the feminine contemplative is most a contemplative when she is most feminine.

If the concept some have of St. Clare, as of contemplatives in general, is that of remoteness, the truth of the matter is that her and their true meaning is faith and love, that faith which is the glory of a woman and that love which is the whole intent of her nature. We agree that grace builds on nature;

and it is the nature of woman to have faith, faith in man who has been set above her and whose helpmate she was created to be, faith in God who made her so to be. This is evident in the life of any normal woman outside convent walls. The extremist may argue for equality of the sexes in *all* things, and even hasten to point out her superiority and dominative powers, but the normal woman knows that a *certain kind* of subjection is her glory.

The greatness of a man can usually be measured by the kind of woman who loves him. Often it is the faith of the woman who loves that discovers and then sustains the greatness of the man. A woman consecrated to God loses none of her natural womanly qualities. At least, she should not. She should only rediscover them on a higher plane. Men conceive ideals. Women make ideals practicable. Men dream great dreams. Women clothe dreams with life and cling to them with faith through all vicissitudes. Stubbornness of faith is one of God's most magnificent gifts to womankind.

St. Francis of Assisi conceived the ideal which has come to bear his name, the Franciscan ideal. Even when it seemed in some degree to fail among men, it consistently and persistently succeeded among women. If it wavered elsewhere, it worked at St. Clare's monastery of San Damiano. And when Francis himself seemed to waver, heartsick and weary with compromise and gloss, he went to Clare and rediscovered himself in her. For this is what she always was: the mirror of Francis' first ideal, first faith, first dream. And she mirrored him because she loved him with all her heart. To be afraid to love is to disqualify oneself for being a true contemplative. For a nun of St. Clare, it is to fail utterly in being her true daughter.

In the close confines of the cloister where human nature

finds no ready-made subterfuges for its defects and where its miseries are all too obvious, love comes to a crossroads sooner or later. It can only be faith which will turn love down the right road of that womanly compassion which is rooted in humility and self-knowledge, the very things the neurotic god cannot abide; and steer love away from that other road of self-righteousness which can even degenerate further into cynicism and end in complete lovelessness, the final triumph of the neurotic god. Faith preserved Clare's love from the peril of ceasing to expect great things of people because people sometimes appeared very small. It made her strong to go on loving them. And it gave her that proper balance of love which is most womanly. Clare knew how to be so gentle as to roam about the little monastery of San Damiano on cold pre-midnights to make sure her sleeping daughters were adequately blanketed. Yet, she had the sternness that could rebuke a nun she miraculously cured of a throat ailment with the very realistic reminder that if the nun did not change her line of conduct some worse ailment was likely to befall her. Here is the love of a true and balanced woman, strong in faith, loving the "black but beautiful" which we, too, must love and which we also are.

Along with the misdirected efforts to hack away at one's womanly nature and set up as a goal a remote and loveless caricature of womanhood, neurotic variations will often appear of that cramped and unreal spirituality which affects a love of being despised and holds suspect, if it does not despise, being loved by others. Any honest woman will admit that she loves to be loved. As a matter of fact, it is usually those who are most healthily aware of their unworthiness to be loved by others who are most frankly grateful to be loved nonetheless. St. Peter urged our Lord to depart from him because he was a sinful man, but we know as well as the Lord knew that St. Peter did not really mean it.

In our best moments of fidelity to spiritual light and grace, we know we are worthy of nothing but the disgust of our companions and the withdrawal of God. At such times, it can be a real luxury to experience a little ill-treatment. But the contemplative must, at the end, relinquish the bizarre comfort of feeling herself despised; she must forego that very authentic if fantastic consolation of others' scorn or disregard. This she exchanges for the joyous anguish of knowing herself loved by God beyond measure. And this is the balance which is the despair of the neurotic god.

It is this very exchange which begets the abiding sorrow for sin which has about it nothing of the sensational, but which is fecund with humility and peace. In a number of current cautionary essays against neuroticism in religious, we find careful explanations of the guilt complex. We are told that real guilt, the guilt of a healthy mind, must be proportionate to the sin committed, so that if I steal one dollar, I regret it with the regret proportionate to one dollar. And after I have stolen a million dollars, I am to be (it is devoutly hoped) regretful of a million-dollar offense. These writers remind us that it would be neurotic to feel the guilt for a million-dollar crime when I had committed only a one-dollar theft. And they are right. They are logical. They are reasonable. To grow in the contemplative life, however, must often mean to transcend reason. That saturation of the soul with God which should be the perfectly normal result of contemplative prayer produces reactions and affords perspectives which can never contradict reason but which will frequently surpass it.

Thus, a contemplative who has spent many years in the cloister has an entirely different outlook on this "guilt" than has a very young religious. While the novice may do well to jot down her failings or her successes-via-grace, to analyze the reasons for her failures to practise virtue or for bogging down in given situations, this could scarcely be the normal kind of examen for an older nun. With the passage of years and perseverance in prayer, there will be no need for examining at the examen. Any deliberate fault will stand out like black ink on white satin, even any half-deliberate fault. They will not need any summoning. Yet neither will they be obsessive.

An older contemplative has a *sense* of guilt, a *sense* of sorrow, rather than a dollar-per-dollar mental set-up. And because she is trying to be faithful to contemplative prayer, the guilt-reaction she experiences for what might objectively be considered a "small fault" is simply a thing that cannot be explained to those who have not experienced it. There is nothing neurotic about feeling, for example, a burning sense of shame for the curiosity we have indulged so genteeley, so subtly. Maybe it involved only an oblique question to discover something we secretly wanted to know and which it is actually not at all out of order for us to know. But the contemplative knows she has been untrue to the exquisite suggestion of grace. And so she is sorry, a million dollars' worth, not the penny's worth that the psychiatrist could rightly insist is objectively proper to the fault.

The aggregate of many such things tends to produce in her that sense of guilt which is not only not neurotic, but is the healthiest thing in the world and actually the greatest threat to the reign of a neurotic god. It is healthy because it is so humbling. She does not brood over her failings, but she is made smaller by them in the sense that God somehow becomes "larger" in her life. The real abiding sorrow for sin is a bowing of the head, not a chewing of the lip. It is a very humbling, cleansing thing. And it is the most normal thing in the spiritual life that the closer the union with God who dwells in light inaccessible, the more monstrous what might scientifically be called a speck appears. Would it not, in fact, indicate a deplorable lack of normal contemplative maturing if "guilt" in this sense retained its first status quo?

Similarly we read good sensible reminders that real guilt attaches itself to a definite object, whereas neurotic guilt attaches itself to no particular object. This is true, of course. Yet, again, we must make distinctions. This is a sound premise, but God is not bound by human premises as He leads a soul into the unfathomable mysteries of His love, or a religious into the mystery of her vocation. For her, the abiding sorrow for sin which is indistinguishable from her active love and is part of her preparation for the graces of passive prayer is unreal and unfruitful precisely when it *does* attach itself to a particular object or objects which give reason for a feeling of guilt. In her case, this would be only unhealthy remorse, whereas it is just exactly the atmospheric particular-object-less sorrow for sin which is at the heart of the cloistered life of penance and prayer.

The contemplative becomes increasingly aware of the burden of sin without reading any particular scales. The deeper her union with God, the more does she perceive the guilt in her own and all the world's betrayals of grace. Just so, the less is she conscious of the particular betrayal. She does not remorsefully dwell on this sin or that fault, hers or the world's. She no longer lists the names and addresses of her failings and keeps visiting them with specific acts of contrition. But her sense of guilt and her sense of sin, her abiding sorrow that God has been offended, grows as details are seen as less meaningful. This is the healthiest frame of mind and state of soul that a contemplative could have. Such a one is no client of the neurotic god and not equipped to become his victim. She knows what is real and what is unreal. At the end of "a bad day," she is prostrate in heart over a sense of having failed in love and humbly resolved to love more faithfully tomorrow. But she is not grimly assembling, counting, and assorting the failures, crash by crash.

What heights and what depths there are in St. Benedict Joseph Labre's confession of his sins: "Father, I have not loved God enough." It may have jolted a confessor accustomed to hearing rather different tales than this in the box. But Benedict Joseph had then nearly reached the pinnacle of his human perfection and was all but fully ripe for death's plucking. He could not list a particular sin. He could not scratch up one deliberate fault. Yet he had a tremendous and profound sense of guilt, an abiding sorrow for sin rather than for sins, so that it was only proper that he should weep with consuming sorrow when he confessed, "I have not loved God enough."

Within each of us is the material for perfect holiness. Otherwise a just God could not have urged us to be perfect as our heavenly Father is perfect. With God is grace. The working and welding of grace and nature will alone produce the saint. The ignoring of either, the rejection of either, will produce the neurotic. In a cloister, it will more likely produce her in that worst of forms, the chronic form, which is the respectable, unsensational, and quite deadly withdrawal from reality, whether it be the withdrawal from her individual self, her womanhood, or the mystery of her vocation.

It is always May in the cloister in a sense, for youth comes each year anew into its old arms and walks under its ancient arches. A seasonal May become static would quickly lose its charm. It is the promise of May which beguiles us, which quickens our hearts and renews our souls each springtime. In the same way, a youthful bud of spirituality cannot remain a bud. If it does not open, it will wither on the monastic stem. A bud is exquisite because it promises a flower. A soul is precious beyond price because it was created to fulfil its destiny of perfection. It must yield its full powers up to God's love.

However zealously the neurotic god preaches the Heresy of the Wrong Direction and utters his blasphemies that God has erred in His creation and laid on human nature obligations which can never be fulfilled, set goals which cannot possibly be realized, still the simple message of the true God will drown that nagging voice unless we are resolved to be nagged. We need not live in a never-never world unless we choose.

And so Pauline this May morning moves to the grate where her sunlight hair will be cut off and flung down before the Lord. It will not be a symbol of doffing her womanhood, but of consecrating her virginal womanhood to God. This is why she will say aloud for her parents, the nuns, all the people present to hear: "It is Thou who wilt restore my inheritance to me." *My* inheritance. The fulfilment of myself which is Your infinitely beautiful plan, O my God.

9

The Neurotic God at Work

"Let those who have received the grace of working labor faithfully," says St. Clare. There is so much wisdom encased in so few and such simple words that it is possible to underestimate the wisdom for the very ease of manner. Work is a grace, Clare insists. And grace is a gift of God. This is already to have a fresh and specialized attitude toward work. For gifts, any but the churl or the boor is grateful. But why, then, is it sometimes difficult to be grateful for work? Difficult for religious who are neither churls nor boors, but dedicated souls sincerely desiring to be united with God? Why is work at times oppressive and even in certain cases a major problem for a religious?

There is no attitude current in the world which does not in some form penetrate convent and cloister walls. A false concept of work spawns multiple heresies, and the neurotic god smiles on them all. According to the difference between persons among his prospective converts, he encourages flight from work or submersion in work. He is delighted when work dominates a worker. He is pleased at another worker's devious methods of casting off the burden of work without appearing to do so. The one thing that makes him sway on his throne is the concept of work as a grace.

When any person, and especially a religious, envisions work as a privilege, approaches it with reverence, embraces it with neither perfunctory politeness nor burning infatuation, but with expectant love, the neurotic god feels sick with frustration. Such a person is not good material for his perfecting into a neurotic. Yet, this very person with the right concept, the reverent approach, the proper zeal, can run into many problems with work and become involved in a number of minor and a few major miseries regarding it. So, the neurotic god rallies his forces and bides his time. Maybe he will get her yet.

Before considering a few matters proper to active religious, we had better define what we mean by the term in the present context. All religious are active in the deepest sense of the word. When Mary sat at the feet of our Lord and was encouraged by Him to remain there even though Martha's soup was boiling over and the potatoes were burning, she was not inactive. Christ did not praise her for sitting on the floor, but for being consciously, actively, at His feet. She was given His solemn word that her kind of work would not be taken away from her because it was a *work* and not an idle repose.

The repose of contemplation is the perfection of activity, when the active powers of the soul fall slack under the hand of God, when activity has reached a peak beyond which it cannot go. Passivity is the highest form of activity, that is, the point at which activity ceases. And when a soul is granted the graces of passive prayer, it has not dropped off to sleep, even in those stages where it may appear to sleep to all things outside its awareness of God. It is doing a great work for God, for itself, and for all souls everywhere. God is acting on it, and the soul is responding with the cessation of its own activity.

Then again, as in His blessed passion and death Christ was passive under the will of His Father and the actions of men and *thus* accomplished the greatest of all acts, the act of Redemption, the supreme salvific work, so does the contemplative soul act in the manner most proper to her vocation when she is passive beneath the action of God in all the details of her life. A contemplative religious is not a perpetual somnabulist through life. She is supposed to be doing something for the Church and for society. She has been entrusted with a tremendous work, and St. Clare expects her to use her "grace of working" here as much as in the chores and activities of her exterior life.

So, when we draw a few distinctions between active and contemplative religious, we do not mean the kind of activity, the kind of awareness of responsibility to God and to society, which is common to both and certainly proper to both, although differently expressed. Here, we mean religious engaged in an exterior apostolate such as teaching or nursing, as distinguished from religious engaged exclusively in an apostolate of contemplative prayer and penance.

These active Sisters are often overburdened with work. This is manifestly and painfully true, despite the best efforts of superiors to equalize burdens and reduce pressures. There is simply too much to do and too few to do it. It is a problem. And major superiors of active religious go on valiantly trying to solve it. There are, however, aspects of work as a problem which are common to both active and enclosed religious and to layfolk as well, and which the workers themselves can often do a considerable amount about solving.

On the face of it, it would seem that to be dominated by one's work is the peculiar professional hazard of the driven teacher or the overworked nurse, but not of the cloistered nun with no academic classes to prepare, no surgeries listed, no state boards to take. The face of it, maybe. But the blood-and-bone truth of it is that the tendency of work to dominate the worker is as much and as formidable a threat in cloisters as out of them. To keep one's life uncluttered is as difficult inside as outside enclosure walls. As a matter of fact, in cloisters, too, there is usually too much to do and too few to do it; but this is not quite the point we want to make here. That point is the responsibility of the individual to preserve the integrity of her dedication in her work.

Here, again, St. Clare has something to say. "Let the Sisters labor . . . in such a way that, while idleness, the enemy of the soul, is banished, they may not extinguish the spirit of holy prayer and devotion, to which other temporal things should be subservient." It is the spirit of prayer which is to be dominant in all things. If it is to be, then obviously the worker must not be dominated by her work.

Now it is just as possible and quite as easy to become submerged in cultivating large gardens as in cultivating the minds of the young. We can be as much overwhelmed by canning, drawing, or dusting as by medical internship. And, in the end, instead of calmly and humbly striving for perfection, we can be dominated by a false concept of perfection as an exacting slave-master.

As the neurotic god sorts out his material in a community, he sets aside one group for specialized indoctrination. These are the religious who can never say "enough." They are eager to serve, determined to "fall to dust in His service," in the felicitous phrase of a modern mystic, willing to take on more and more activities for the good of the community. By encouraging them, he sets up an excellent pretense of doing the work of the true God. For certainly we should give ourselves to the service of God in the service of the community. The neurotic god whispers heartening words to these religious as they multiply their activities to the point where the day cannot hold them. When it cannot, there is nothing to do but move faster and faster. This also failing, there will next be corners to cut on prayer in the choir. Unpunctualities will begin to multiply. The day's duties will start creeping into the morning meditation. Walking to the choir for the Office will become less a time for gently calling together one's spiritual forces for the great work of chanting the praises of God than one for planning what we shall do as soon as the chanting is over.

Little by little, the best kind of material for sanctity can become material for the heresy of activism, the most popular heresy of our age. When a religious arrives at this stage of work pressure, she can accept the heresy and try to justify it with brave talk of service and dedication, and work being prayer. But work, *per se,* is not prayer. What Cardinal Suhard has written of the priest is equally true of the religious: "The priest must not use his goal of tremendous solidarity with mankind as a pretext for abandoning the traditional means of sanctification in favor of a spirituality based on the principle that activity carries its own asceticism with it . . . Prayer, spiritual reading, days of recollection, retreats, adoration of the Blessed Sacrament the rosary, examination of conscience, regular Confession, protracted thanksgiving, well-recited breviary . . . these are spiritual exercises which no priest may neglect, much less abandon, without committing an imprudence whose consequences (have no illusions about it) may make of it a serious sin."[1] And again: "The priest must con-

[1] Emmanuel Cardinal Suhard, *Priests Among Men* (Notre Dame, Indiana, Fides), p. 89.

sider it a very grave error to neglect his own sanctification, and become overly immersed in external works, however holy."[1]

Work can be done, and in the case of a religious it must be done, in a spirit of prayer. It can be an expression of the love of God and a specific means of sanctification. But it is not a synonym, much less a substitute, for either the choral prayer of the Office or the deep contemplative prayer which should be the undivided occupation of the religious at the times set aside for it on the daily schedule. No more is it a substitute for a layman's meditation.

Neither is work to serve as proxy for spiritual reading, any more than it is to be made a substitute for eating. It is strange that many a well-intentioned person will think it quite all right to abort without urgent necessity the precious minutes designated as an immediate preparation for the chanting of the Office, the periods of private meditation or spiritual reading and the like, under the spurious justification that "work is prayer," although no one ever declares that "work is dinner" and then consistently sews or hammers away during the times of repast. Neither does anyone say: "Work is sleep" and proceed to type all night.

We can eat prayerfully and give glory to God while we do it, but the consumption of cabbage is not specifically prayer. We can sleep prayerfully, that is, in obedience and with desire to renew our strength for further service. And thus even a snore can give glory to God. Yet, snoring is not properly prayer. And we can hoe or stitch or sketch or scrub in a state of deep union with God without, however, any of these things assuming *per se* the status of prayer. It is true that prayer is often work and sometimes the hardest kind of work, but we do not find half the community electing to remain before the

[1] *Ibid.*, p. 89.

Tabernacle during spring housecleaning with a smiling avowal that "prayer is work." It is often said, and very well said, that if we pray only in the choir we pray little. To conclude from this, however, that it is not necessary to pray in the choir if only we keep hustling is to be a very confused kind of logician. And to insist that hustling *is* prayer is to contravene St. Clare's injunction and make all things subservient to hustling.

In the early ages of monasticism, periods of mental prayer for the monk or nun were not specified in the daily horarium. It was taken for granted that the religious was more or less engaged in mental prayer all the time. As the weaving of mats went out and the pressures of modern activities came in, it was realized that specific periods of reconnoitering were essential for the religious. The morning and afternoon meditation in the choir became a law of the Church. The spiritual reading which occupied so large a part of the life of monks and nuns of a gentler age became particularly enjoined in the welter of works in which religious must now live. A yearly retreat was insisted upon, and contemplatives were not exempted from the law.

God in His infinite understanding of her desires will surely accept the work of a driven religious as a prayerful outpouring of her love and dedication when she is occasionally obliged to forego the choral Office or the periods of private prayer before the altar. This is not at all the same case as that of the religious who frequently separates herself from the community exercises of prayer with the bland cliché that "work is prayer."

It is the generous religious bemused by this heresy of activism, however, who summons the attention of the neurotic god. Those who continually drive themselves beyond their strength become religious of mounting tensions. They want to do so much for others that they come to have no time for others. They are so determined to serve others that they can grow extremely irritable toward others in their very anxiety to serve them. It is possible to be too busy to help anyone because we are so busy helping everyone. One of the most pathetic figures in religious life is the nun who is tense and cross only because she is continually pressuring herself to be all things to all men beyond the limits of her capacity. And she is the darling of the neurotic god because he hopes to curdle her generous dispositions by the tensions he knows so well how to induce.

What is the solution? Probably it is repeated failure, educational failure from which we gather the widsom which is in itself success. Theorizing about the ideal religious community in which work is evenly proportioned so that no one is ever driven and no one ever deprived of prayer time in the choir or leisure on Sundays, where the schedule is always inviolably followed by all, and where the sun sets each evening on a group of smiling women who have finished a tidy day's work and tucked it in with a sense of satisfaction, fulfillment, and accomplishment, is poor theorizing, primarily because that would not be an ideal community, even if it did exist. The best community is certainly not the self-satisfied community, any more than the best religious is the nun who can solve all her problems with facility and finality.

However, it is well worth taking the time we think we do not have to examine very sincerely how many of all these pressures and tensions we continually read about, and perhaps experience, are exterior pressures and how much of it all is avoidable interior pressure. In the name of service, we can frenziedly carry through many a project which is actually highly dispensable, but is a pet project of our own determination.

That a religious, or a layman for that matter, should have many desires to serve which time and energy do not permit that person to realize is no basis for frustration. It is perfectly normal and, especially for the religious, a means of hidden self-denial and humility. To bow before external restrictions or personal limitations can require far more virtue than to twirl through life in a perpetual hurricane, raising much dust but little else. Each person, religious obedience or no religious obedience, assignments or no assignments, commitments or no commitments, and despite the contrary insistence of the neurotic god who wants his clients to keep at their hustling, abort their praying, and abandon their thinking, has to establish some kind of hierarchy of values in the works of his hands and the works of his mind. This is part of solving the work problem. After it is done, there will be problems enough remaining. These are for God to solve.

June is a month of intensity. In Roswell, it is usually the month of intensest heat and often of intensest work. The fields are ripening, the weeds are thriving, the canning is under way, the summer brides must be outfitted, the new line of greeting cards for sale is being designed, the annual newsletter being set up for printing. Besides these extra-curricular activities, the ordinary work of the monastery continues in all details. The choral Office goes on. Spiritual exercises keep their place. And it is hot. Still, June is immemorially the month of love and of brides. Sister Joel was one of our June brides.

After a year of postulate, two years of noviceship, and three of simple vows, Sister Joel had attained years so ripe as to number twenty-four. But on this June morning of her solemn vows, she looked still the determined eighteen-year-old who had patiently waited to enter since she was fifteen. The grey-green eyes were very grave above the little flame of the bridal candle she held as she knelt before the altar and sang her *"Suscipe me."* After she pronounced her solemn vows, she began immediately the singing of her bridal proclamation: *"Regnum mundi et omnem ornatum saeculi contempsi, propter amorem Domini mei Jesu Christi quem vidi, quem amavi, in quem credidi, quem dilexi."*[1]

The young voice was soft but very firm and sure, as befits the exuberant melody. *"Suscipe me"* is a slow-moving, solemn rhythm. *"Regnum mundi"* is a lilting lyric which snaps its melodic fingers at all the allurements of the world piled together. What are these compared with the Lover whom she sees by faith, whom she loves, in whom she believes, whom she has chosen above all because He has first loved and chosen her? The choir caught up the joy of the bride and joined in: "My heart has uttered a good word; I speak my works to the King!"

Immediately after that, the wedding ring was placed on Sister Joel's finger and a crown of thorns upon her head while the priest prayed that she might merit to share in the Passion of Christ. It is a telling reminder that just as we must become worthy to be free, so also we must merit to suffer. And here may be the only certain clue to the problem of work, as here may be the one definitive answer to the neurotic god at work. "I speak my works to the King." And I work with thorns encircling my head. Another translation has it: "I speak my poem to the King." Work considered as a poem has its profound significance, too, and the same crown of thorns around its head. The thorny crown will not remain materially upon the head of the young religious, but it will remain there in a spiritual sense. It will be hung over her bed in her little cell for a

[1] "The kingdom of earth and all the grandeur of the world I have despised for the love of my Lord Jesus Christ whom I have seen, whom I have loved, in whom I have believed, whom I have chosen above all."

symbol and a sign, and she and it will grow old together. Only when she dies will thorns cease to have significance for her. Then they will wreathe flowers around her head.

Not to be dominated by work requires that we step out of our work. Our plans and our pressures, our assorted activities, commitments and deadlines, exhibit a new dimension when we say to ourselves: "Thou fool! This night they shall require thy soul of thee!" That silly fellow of whom Scripture tells that he was lining up his future by the bundle and the bale, with death already tapping him on the shoulder, was actually no more foolish than those doing the same with activities. It can be a highly effective tranquillizer for a harassed and pressured worker to step back from the harassments and the pressures and remind herself: "You fool! This night they shall require your soul of you!" For, as a matter of fact, this night, this day, this hour and this moment, God does require her soul of her. And it is all He requires. It is our mistake to think He requires success or completion.

In the name of striving for perfection, we can render ourselves slaves of abstract perfection. God requires of us our soul, our living soul coming up against the unexpected and unforeseen, the uncategorized trials, the puzzlements and bewilderments and complexities of demands that sometimes press in from four directions with equal imperiousness. It is not a theory of perfection which God requires. If it were merely a case of finding pat solutions to problems of work and applying them, there would actually be no problems. We all incline toward the remedy which says: "Apply generously, allow to dry, polish." But in the works we daily speak to the King, we very often do not, cannot, and perhaps *ought not* to know what to apply or allow to dry. And so, thank God, we never feel polished. Thank God, because we may be closest to perfection, which is union with God, when we are most painfully aware of being thoroughly unpolished; farthest from it when we are feeling, let us say it, rather shiny, really.

The countless small frustrations that arise in daily work are often the very material of a deepening union with God. They are His mysterious way of requiring our souls of us. To forego the satisfaction of ever doing a piece of work with the perfection *we* should like, of ever performing it in leisurely detail, lacking time for the desired "finish," is one of the most searching forms of self-denial. What enchants the neurotic god is the sight of a tired religious beating her mental and emotional fists against frustrations and pressures. It enchants him because sooner or later, and probably sooner, a fissure is going to open in her mind and her emotions. And then she will be his.

A grape, after all, needs to be pressed if it is to become wine. A religious may require to be frustrated so that she does not become infatuated with activity. After we have momentarily, and at what frequent intervals may be indicated, stepped back and out of our work and whispered in our own heart: "Fool! This moment He requires your *soul* of you," we may want to embrace the frustrations. Nothing could more appall the neurotic god.

Yet, suppose we believe this, try to do it, and repeatedly fail? Is it a sign that the theory is invalid? More likely it is a sign that we are learning to succeed in the only way many of us can,—by repeated failures. A nun knows that the tensions of an overloaded work day must be controlled and relaxed. She understands that irritability and impatience when she is hard-pressed contribute nothing to the situation except to worsen it. How well Father Henri de Lubac has said that patience is the elder sister of efficiency! She wants to work

prayerfully, recollectedly. Yet, she finds the tension mounting. She becomes increasingly irritable. And the only prayer
she can manage is a setting of her teeth against impatient words.
She feels she has failed again. It may be that God feels
differently. To make the same mistakes over and over again is
sometimes the only way to learn compassion and the only
approach to humility. Edith Stein in Carmel had often to
check herself with: "Easy, Edith, easy now!"

Our theory is not wrong or even suspect because we are too
weak and imperfect to act on it at all times. "I speak my works
to the King," the choir sings with Sister Joel. But it is thorns,
not roses, that are placed on her head. The nun who seems to
herself to fail quite consistently may be the most successful nun
in the community. She cannot keep the details of her life in
good order. She cannot solve all the little problems of work or
the large problem of activity. But why do we have this quaint
notion that problems must always be completely solved? God
has never required this. He merely requires our soul of us.
The question of whether He is more glorified by a flawless or
a mediocre work performance is one He alone can answer.
Problems are always to be suffered, but not always to be
solved. It is a point worth remembering when, even for the
contemplative, the problem of keeping calm in the press of
activities arises; when she does not know how to reconcile St.
Paul's "the charity of Christ urges us" (2 Cor. v,14) with a
tight work schedule, and cannot determine a balance between
giving herself to the usurers and accomplishing her duties;
when the love in her heart demands to be expressed in services she has not the time to perform.

Discussion of the problems of work for the religious, as also
for the layman desiring to lead an integrated spiritual life,
involves walking a kind of mental tightrope. A superior is

bound to strive for an equalization of work within the community, to help each religious realize her potential so as to be a fruitful branch on the community tree, to prevent in what measure she can perpetual frustrations in an office or a charge, and make it difficult for the neurotic god to get his toe in the door. Yet it is often so very difficult to do all this. Superiors must see that the rule is kept and still understand that sometimes and in certain circumstances its letter cannot be. They are guardians of discipline, but they are also spiritual mothers of human daughters and not engineers of automatons. One of their first duties will be to look to capabilities. If it is wrong for a subject to covet and bid for certain work and to skirt the chores she dislikes, it is also a fatal mistake for the superior to impose burdens that obviously cannot be borne. If we do not come to the monastery to do what we like to do, neither shall we normally be contented and balanced religious if we are continually put at work for which we are entirely unfitted.

St. Colette walks the tightrope with enviable grace in her constitutions. It was no fireside philosopher but a very practical woman who tartly reminded her subjects that bowing out of an unwelcome task with the plea: "I have not received the grace to do it" is merely a false pretense of humility. This same wise mother, however, immediately subjoins on the abbess that she is not to impose work which she knows or well suspects a nun is not equipped to perform. The old idea of making religious life a perpetual thwarting of the subject's desires and potential has reached the point of senility. It is one of the great beauties of community life that each nun contributes her full measure to its operation. When even one member does not, there is inevitable upset in a community. One of the most excellent qualities in a superior is her affinity with her subjects in this matter. She is a very good mother who understands the resources and the capability of each of her daughters, helping them to plumb the first and realize the other.

No one in a community is all-efficient. The interdependence of its members is characteristic of any normal and happy social unit, and certainly of a normal and happy monastery where each nun is gratefully conscious of her need of all the other nuns. There is no religious who alone has everything to give her community, nor is there any religious who has not something to contribute to the common fund. Long ago, for instance, I discovered the one, if admittedly the only, way in which I am simply indispensable to our community. It is in the matter of household maintenance. I may not be a superb cook like Sister Beatrice nor a prodigious jack-of-all-trades like Sister Celine. I realize I shall never be able to do creative drawing as Sister Benedicta does, nor play the violin as Sister Assumpta plays. I am not an expert gardener like Sister Dolores nor as adept a seamstress as Sister Leo. But just let a domestic tragedy of household maintenance arise, and I am unexcelled. Whether a pipe bursts, the floor furnace gases, the ironer sticks, or the laundry floods, I retain the reassuring calm and poise of the person who has the situation under perfect control. I always know exactly what to do, and I always very promptly do it. I call Sister Juliana.

There was that stirring experience I had at the bathroom sink last year. I opened the faucet and the customary trickle which is all our ancient and corroded pipes were able to produce dribbled unenthusiastically down. I closed the faucet. There was no cessation of the trickle. I swung the handle again and turned it firmly off. The trickle ominously increased in volume. I felt the strange fright which those who have been reared in an atmosphere of respectful admiration for plumbing feel when plumbing suddenly fails them. I swung the faucet again. The handle now could be twirled completely and uninhibitedly around full circle. This both appalled and fascinated me. I swung it around a score of times, as panic mounted. Faucets do not behave like this, my subconscious contributed. And after twenty years in the monastery and having been trained since my postulant days never, never to waste water, I watched the gathering trickle slipping down the drain with anguish. The reason I did not cry out in my anguish was that it was the great silence. Another complication. But then my customary balance in domestic crises reasserted itself. I walked determinedly to Sister Juliana's cell and rapped meaningfully at the door.

True to the great silence, we spoke no word. I beckoned. She followed. I pointed dramatically at the faucet. She regarded it thoughtfully and fingered it speculatively. Sister Juliana looks too calm, I thought. She does not realize the impact of this affair. With a slighly reproachful wave of my hand at the water going wastefully down the drain, I gently edged her fingers off the faucet. I would show her. I would bring the situation home to her. I twirled the handle completely around half a dozen times, stood back, and indicated with a broad and tragic gesture: See

Still looking what I considered inappropriately tranquil, Sister Juliana gave a slight shrug and turned back toward her cell. "Coward!" I thought. If she supposes she is going to leave me to a solitary vigil with this diabolic faucet, she is a victim of illusion. I made a grab for her habit sleeve. Sister Juliana smiled her sweet smile and made the monastic sign for "just a minute!" I kept watch at the sink, trying to calculate how many quarts of water had now been wasted, until Sister Juliana returned with some curious baggage.

Now the only reason I have ever wished I were an archbishop is so that I could have the local visitation of the monastery and discover how many secret panels Sister Juliana has in her cell. It is a very small cell. Yet, along with three boards and a straw sack, a washstand and a bench, Sister Juliana keeps assorted and exotic equipment for handling any household emergency. As maintenance problems arise, weapons to deal with them marvelously proceed from this mysterious cell. The night of The Possessed Faucet, Sister Juliana emerged with several small boards and a fascinating assortment of corks. I watched her fit various corks into the mouth of the faucet, while the frustrated little flow of water spurted angrily up her arm. I regarded her pokings and proddings with a mixture of respect and disbelief in their efficacy.

She twisted and pushed, enlisted me to help push, forced a board against the corked faucet, fitted a small platform board under the first board, and then raised the platform with still another board. Even when not pushing, I was by no means idle. Although hampered by the restrictions of the great silence, I managed to convey by doleful shakes of the head, sharp intakes of breath, and gentle wringing of the hands that this could not possibly work. However, it did work, as Sister Juliana's home plumbing does invariably work.

Next day the plumber came. I was acting as portress and heard his admiring remarks. "Say, that was pretty smart," he volunteered, sizing up the corks, platform and supporting beam. He turned to me and said with professional respect, "You do that?" Temptation was violent to lower my eyelashes and murmur modestly: "Really, my good fellow, it was nothing." But grace triumphed. "No sir," I said, "one of the other nuns is very clever about fixing things."

Actually, every nun is clever about something, if it is only in recognizing, rejoicing in and assisting the cleverness of others. It is the office of the superior to discover the something.

It is the business of subjects to pool their energies and abilities into a smooth-flowing common endeavor. And part of any nun's service to her community, as well as any layman's to his, is to appreciate the value of others. It is sometimes a temptation to superiors as well as to older religious to misproportion work by continually increasing the load of the quick and efficient not only at their expense but also at the expense of the slower ones not included in new undertakings and not entrusted with responsibility. In the end, such procedures are followed at the expense of the entire community. It may be true that "to get a thing done, ask a busy man," but sometimes people must be educated to get things done and even taught to be busy.

So, the superior must walk her tightrope, endeavoring to use all the resources of the energetic—but not beyond their capacity—trying to rouse potential drifters to greater efforts, and to encourage and develop those who feel inferior, balancing work and prayer so that all temporal things are ever subservient to the spirit of prayer, and waging a maternal war against the neurotic god of work. As the subject must repeatedly step back and out of her work in order not to be dominated by it, so the superior must repeatedly enter more profoundly into the mystery of her office and discover new depths of her spiritual motherhood. Tightropes can be walked with grace and ease by expert walkers. And the balancing rod here, as everywhere in religious life, is prayer. That is why, in problems of work, the neurotic god always proposes a wringing of the hands and omission of prayer in the choir.

Work is such a clean and healthy and wholesome thing, but the neurotic god knows how to overseason it, curdle it, vitiate it. Once her work dominates a religious, she is grist for the mill of the neurotic god. Sometimes a calm reassessment of our busyness reveals surprising things. Perhaps our pride has blinded us to the extent that we cannot realize that a work imperfectly done for sheer objective lack of time is not so much for our present humiliation as for our eternal glory. "I speak my works to the King," not to men. If there can be large frustrations in work which superiors are obliged to remove as far as they can, there are many and maybe even legion minor frustrations in work that are the result of pride, impatience, irritability, officiousness,—any of that long train that we tend to euphemize as "nervousness." It can at times be a most efficacious confession and the simultaneous defeat of the neurotic god to admit frankly to oneself: I am cross today. I am tired. I only lack the wings to qualify as a wasp. And I am not going to translate this into the international idiom of excuse and say that "I am nervous today." Perhaps no word has been so flung about and misused as "nervousness." Lack of virtue and nervousness are not the same thing.

Fatigue is nearly always a problem in religious life. With the regular night rising, the exacting penance and the restrictions of the cloistered life, it can be a perennially vexing problem for the contemplative. Here again is the tightrope. We have to learn how far and how justifiably zeal and mortification can push back the frontiers of extreme fatigue. Weariness can be a deeply interior oblation to God when a religious works doggedly on, without spirit, without energy, and sometimes with a tired sense of the meaninglessness of everything. And often God marvelously rewards such an oblation so that the religious who pushed on when it seemed nearly impossible is mysteriously refreshed and renewed. St. Teresa of Avila remarked how, when she persevered in prayer against the importunings of fatigue, she was often reinvigorated afterwards not only in spirit but in body as well. These things do not happen to saints alone.

Yet, the just demands of nature must be respected and to some extent granted. Against the efforts of the neurotic god to encourage a religious to run faster and faster until she falls and breaks an emotional arm is set the grace of God who is the only final solution to our uncertainties and our problems. The will of God is seldom unequivocally made known to us with neat underscorings. At least for the contemplative, it seems often to be the will of God that she should not know what the will of God is. And this is a very wonderful thing, that because we are ever unsure, ever awaiting His further word, we have to cling so closely to Him and to lean so heavily on His arm. If she stops to consider the matter, the beloved will surely prefer clinging to the Lover each hour of the day, to getting clear briefing and despatch for the day once each morning. This is part of that same reassessment indicated above.

It is a bad thing to be frustrated always. It may be a good thing to be frustrated sometimes. We do not need an immediate certainty about every situation and detail of life as long as we have the radical certainty that we speak our works to the King. Unfinished work, overpowering work, driving work is still spoken to the King. And because He requires only our soul of us, those dreary adjectives will be quite meaningless in His eyes, except insofar as they can be sincerely translated as testimonials of love for Him. God has never asked us to succeed. This is only what we demand of ourselves. It is what the neurotic god insists upon.

And he also insists that we have to figure things out. We have to get organized. Something has to be done. Problems must be completely solved. His victory over his followers is to throw them into minor or major emotional frenzy with the figuring, organizing, doing, and solving. All the time, God is there, Himself the answer, the order, the act, and the solution. Often our share in the solution is merely a matter of gaining perspective. And proper perspectives are not gained in a welter of doing but in the silence of prayer.

St. Pius X had good advice for a priest too busy to make his half-hour morning meditation. "Make your meditation for an hour, my son."

The neurotic god gets tremendously excited about work. He insists on objective perfection, although it does not really exist. He chews his nails. He does not sleep well, even though he has chased in fast circles around, and inside, the choir all day. He worries incessantly. He has to do these things, for he must be a model for his proselytes. But he never works with a symbolic crown of thorns on his head. And his works are not spoken to the King.

10

The Neurotic God at Play

July 16 is St. Clare's birthday. This year she is seven hundred and seventy years old, and it must be admitted that she is holding up rather well. After bearing thousands and thousands of spiritual daughters over a period of more than seven centuries, Clare is still as fresh and vibrant and lovely as when her monastic family consisted of two: herself and her solitary subject, Agnes, her younger sister.

In the cloister, nuns do not celebrate the anniversary of their arrival into the world but of their arrival into the spiritual marriage of vows. It is a nun's wedding anniversary, the date of her profession, along with her nameday, which are days of festivity for her on which the other nuns take extra loving pains to show their affection for her. But with the mother foundress it is different. What a day it was for the Poor Clares when St. Clare was born! And so July 16 means specialized song and prayer, particular spiritual thanksgiving and rejoicing. And, in Roswell, it means The Picnic.

We have never been able to persuade the neurotic god to come to The Picnic. He is above this type of frivolity. In fact, he sternly disapproves of it. He should. For it might be his undoing. Instead, he takes a tranquillizer, sits on his aluminum throne, and makes observations on The Picnic.

In the first place, the ripples of excitement preceding it disgust him. One day, one meal, out of all the year, the nuns are going to talk while they eat. The neurotic god is well up on the rule. He knows it forbids recreation in the refectory during meals. And he wishes that on July 16 the nuns would stay in the refectory and not go out on the lawn or the porch, abandoning a proper monastic meal in favor of this ridiculous picnic collation. One year they even planned to have the picnic at the burial vault. That was the time the neurotic god had to take triple aspirin and remain in bed.

It would be bad enough if the teen-aged postulants got excited about a picnic, but that the older nuns should spend several recreation periods before the fateful July 16 animatedly planning details of the picnic instead of studying the latest manoeuvres of their psyches,—this is quite intolerable. Contemplative nuns, committed to an enclosed life of penance and prayer, and here they are, inquiring of the abbess whether there will be movies (by which is meant still colored slides from some other monastery) at the picnic! Stephen Foster's "Lemuel" and "Glendy Burke" are rewritten by Sister Beatrice and vigorously practised at recreation with enthusiastic applause at the "we'll work no more today" refrain. Sister Benedicta reports dire leaks in some of the paper cups which were washed and stored away from last year's picnic, and Sister Elizabeth suggests writing to the company in protest at paper cups whose life span does not cover three or four years. Sister Assumpta bitterly recalls the time she was drenched from an aged paper cup whose seams had parted at the last washing, unbeknown to her, and demands that all picnic equipment this year be inspected by the state safety commission. "Lofty interchange indeed," observes the neurotic god as he helps himself to another phenobarbital.

And then there is the thing itself, the picnic. After Vespers, rosary, and meditation, when the neurotic god might expect the nuns to be properly sober and preferably sad of countenance, they gather in a tight circle around the abbess, invoke the Holy Spirit upon their recreation, and then erupt onto the lawn, looking really unpardonably gay. He is reminded of C. S. Lewis' observation in a Screwtape letter that "the phenomenon of joy is of itself disgusting and a direct insult to the realism, dignity, and austerity of hell."[1] It is unfortunate, of course, that Mr. Lewis made this little slip of writing "hell" where, in the neurotic god's opinion, he should have written "adult life."

Imagine nuns expecting the Holy Spirit to preside at a gathering like this! The conversation alone, my dear! Sister Dolores demands public confession from the party who broke two of the three teeth off this plastic fork last year, and then subsides miserably when Mother Abbess says that *she* did and what about it? Sister Beatrice and Sister Joel arrive from the kitchen with the sandwiches amid welcoming cries. There is prolonged haranguing over the discovery that the community has now grown to such extent that equipment includes only one small plastic knife for every two or three nuns. Sister Leo quiets this uprising with a salutary reminder not to be so fussy and to stop putting on airs. She remembers picnics when they had none of these new-fangled utensils.

The nuns hike around the garden, the same garden they see every day of their lives. They sing rounds and applaud themselves vigorously. They play blockflutes and listen with burn-

[1] *The Screwtape Letters* (New York, Macmillan).

ing appreciation to the supplement to the Martyrology written by Sister Assumpta and prophetically setting down the details of the earthly exodus of the present community members. Sister Benedicta will be thrown into the Pecos River with a Latin dictionary tied about her neck. Sister Margaret will be immersed in scalding oatmeal, only to emerge more vigorous than before, in the manner of St. John before the Latin Gate energetically shaking off the drops of boiling oil and getting on with his business. Thrifty Sister Elizabeth will be heard to gasp: "Turn off the light," as she slips the bonds of earth.

After more of this kind of thing, the neurotic god feels it is time to start writing up case histories. *Lack of Mental Development among Cloistered Nuns,* he puts down with firm underscoring; *Result # 1, Depression.* But then he hears another insurrection of laughter and hastily crosses out "depression." *Inability to Face Reality: Escapism.* That's better. But by this time his mentally underdeveloped patients are interestedly facing the reality of cheese sandwiches and escaping down curls of potato chips.

Now let it be vehemently agreed at once that there is nothing amusing about neuroticism. Mental illnesses, emotional disturbances, psychic deviations are matters to evoke our deep compassion and elicit all the help the sufferers can be given. There are many excellent psychiatrists who are working with sincerest dedication to help victims of neurosis to help themselves. Reorientations are often successfully made and deserve the applause of our prayers. Reorientations are also often not achieved, and this is matter for our persevering prayer and effort. There is an imposing mass of literature available on the subject, much of it written by highly competent and experienced professional men and women. There is also, however, a great deal of nonsense written on the subject by obviously incompetent and ill-experienced persons. In this type of outpouring, neuroticism is made to appear rather chic. The fact is that psychosis, neurosis and all their progeny have become quite the rage. They are pacesetters. And the pace they are setting for many a religious is false, perverted, and destructive.

Judging from the volume of psychiatric effusions in current journals, many a religious journal among them, the innocent bystander could well conclude that there is something definitely wrong with a balanced, unproblematical, happy religious. She is not in the swim. She is out of step with the times. She ought to see her psychiatrist, except that she does not have one. Normalcy has come to be so suspect that if a nun upholds the worth of old penitential practices, she is a sadistic introvert. If she cherishes her religious habit, she is a reactionary. If she understands the function of customs in religious life and sees a value in symbols, she is unadult

We need not be exceptionally erudite historians to have observed that every upsurge of good in the Church as in secular society has gathered the inevitable froth of extremism on it. When Satan cannot defeat a good, he makes friends with it. And his friendship can never mean anything but pollution. The aristocracy at the time of the French Revolution was, by and large, a deplorable comment on humanity. The extremists who butchered the aristocracy were a not less deplorable comment. Evil can never be overcome except by good. Evil is never defeated by evil. In much the same way, good is never made better by destruction, but only by construction. The first requisite for competency to improve a thing is the realization that the thing is already largely or at least partly good. No one tries to improve evil or sin or error, but only to supplant, absolve, or correct them, which is to say, remove them. Yet how easily we become infatuated with a new movement, to the extent that we are swept not so much off our feet as off our head about it and come to confound improvement with total demolition. When we are infatuated, we are totally absorbed to the point where we are ourselves devoured. A person swept off his head is apt to make some very peculiar statements. Thus extremism, while it never effects anything of lasting worth, can be uncommonly destructive for a time. The devil likes nothing better than that people with good intentions start running a high temperature as they set out to do good. Feverish reform, feverish activity, the feverish rally, —these are his delight. Of course, he himself is accustomed to a very hot climate.

As there are some fundamentally well-intentioned unthinkers who are contributing a great deal toward spoiling good Pope John's glorious vision of *"aggiornamento"* by their extremism, so there are determined extremists in this matter of neurotic disturbance, too. What they seem so determined about proving is that normalcy no longer exists. To do this, they must inflate all the little and large anxieties of life, the sufferings which are the inheritance of a fallen race, the everyday problems and perplexities, into heroic-sized assaults on sanity. Even more particularly, they must reduce the many joys with which God brightens our vale of tears to subnormalities.

Every normal rub of individual against individual in community life is not "a personality problem." The life of any religious, as the life of any layman, is always going to include unexpected problems, sufferings, difficult situations. These are not "traumatic experiences." They merely witness to the truth that this *is* a vale of tears and that we have all inherited original sin and its consequences.

The most ordinary terms can be tortured into synonyms for symptoms of psychosis. There is "emotional disturbance," for instance. In using this as a technical term, we may come to forget that it also has a very natural untechnical sense. They should not be, but frequently are, confused. To be emotionally disturbed is often the most telling symptom of normalcy. When I spilled a full bottle of cedar oil down the front of our new Habit, I was definitely emotionally disturbed. Doubtless the Sister who has charge of the Habits was also. When Sister Beatrice feels depressed that her bread did not rise properly and has burned on one side, she is reacting as any normal woman reacts to cookery defeats, and is emotionally disturbed. She is not thereby to be classified as melancholic. Sister Juliana loves the color red. She is emotionally disturbed when she encounters red; that is to say, she is delighted. She likes her red blanket and the red leather cover on her *Liber Usualis*. This would be all some current counsellors would need to work out a theory that Sister Juliana was thwarted as a child and so now she sees red everywhere. She must see red. She is driven to see red. She has a red fixation.

Sister Anne is in an even worse state. She could never tolerate perfumery when she was in the world. In the cloister, she keeps her childhood preference for the smell of gasoline or related odors, sniffing happily when someone is using cleaning fluid or paint remover. Must this be tortured into an indication that Sister Anne has incendiary neurosis?

It is not a happy experience to pick up a religious periodical and read a worried article about the danger of encouraging sexual aberrations among seminarians by allowing them to wear cassocks—that is, skirts. It is, in fact, nauseating. And if we feed our young religious such tainted food we shall richly deserve to have some genuine problem personalities in our communities later on and more emotional disturbance than we could have dreamed.

What kind of thinking wishes to put nuns on the public bathing beach and take the cassocks off our priests and seminarians? There was a time when the neurotic god had to gnaw his way into religious thinking like the termite he is, but on many fronts that time seems definitely past. He is now the guest speaker at many a panel discussion, and normalcy seems to be slipping out of style. St. Teresa of Avila has written of the pendulum swing of mood common to any normal woman who hums on a pulsing spring morning and feels extremely glum when all her cupboards have got into disorder. Teresa remarked that there were days when she felt she could suffer anything at all for our Lord and had proved it, too, as circumstances gave occasion. She added that there were other days when she felt she could not so much as step on an ant for the love of God. It is safe to predict how some modern psychiatric advisers would diagnose Teresa today. Schizophrenia.

St. Clare once refused the provisions brought her nuns by a Franciscan friar. At that particular time, the duty of giving spiritual instruction to the Poor Ladies had been lifted from Franciscan friars by Pope Gregory IX's Bull, *Quo Elongati,* which confirmed the precept forbidding the friars to visit women's convents without permission from the Holy See. Clare was crushed by this, but not too crushed to react as a hot-blooded Italian noblewoman. She dismissed the friars who brought food to the Sisters, saying that if the friars were not to provide spiritual food for her daughters, they need not provide material food, either. This little incident is a particularly telling one as regards the character and personality of St. Clare. What it tells is that she was a woman of strong reactions, and richly gifted with that canny determination characteristic of the feminine species. No man, be he the local Father Guardian or the Bishop of Rome, was likely to sleep well

on the thought of fifty cloistered nuns starving to death, especially if he knew that the leading lady in this drama was a lady
of consummate holiness. Pope Gregory hastily revised his decision and, as is the common instinct in such a situation,
passed on the responsibility. He said the Franciscan Minister-
General should decide these matters. The Poor Ladies got
their instruction and their bread, too.

What we are *not* to conclude from this delightful vignette
in the life of Clare is that she was a frustrated woman who
rebelled at reality and needed psychiatric treatment. She was
a determined woman who knew how to change reality where
a change seemed under God to be indicated.

Again, how many pages have been written to analyze the
perfectly natural reaction of a sensitive and dramatic little girl
to a piece of jelly bread that had gone soggy from delayed
consumption! Because the little girl became St. Therese of
Lisieux, it has been thought necessary to elaborate any childish emotion of hers into a lengthy discourse proving in turn
that she was (a) neurotic, (b) prophetic, (c) psychic. Similarly, if the child next door should be offered a choice of gifts,
only to announce: "I choose everything" and carry off the
entire assortment of merchandise, we would say: "Don't be so
selfish." But it is too embarrassing to find that a great saint was
a very normal little girl. So we say: "Look! Even then she
had universality of spirit! See the limitless desire!" St. Therese
is far too great a woman to need any such false laborings of
common childish reactions. Do we perhaps need to relax a
little in our anxiety to dissect the saints? Is the breath of the
neurotic god getting just a bit too hot on our necks?

We are not helping our real mental sufferers by acting as
though everyone were mentally ill. By what kind of logic do
we conclude, as it has been concluded, that St. Margaret

Mary was neurotic because she disliked cheese? We are certainly not solving problems of neurosis by making neurosis stylish. Incompetent writers, with their tortured approach to the most normal situations in life, tend to discredit the fine work being done by the competent.

In many books and essays coming off our presses with alarming momentum, it seems clear that by appraisal of religious life we can only mean dispraise. Anything done last century is strictly for the incinerator. Any custom fifty years old has to be senile. With this gathering momentum, we are obviously moving toward the climax where anything done last week is outmoded this week. And we are casting a suspicious eye on the sturdiest and happiest traditions of religious life, which is precisely what the neurotic god wishes us to do. This is *his* game.

If the few religious who find community life intolerable happen to be verbose—as they usually are—and articulate—as they occasionally are—this does not alter the fact that they are the few. The mere fact that a book appears lathered with the sweat of its author immediately disqualifies it as unbiased writing. But we have so many books of this type that we may fail to apply our own calm critical faculties to them. Of how much current writing on the religious life could we say, as was said of Peter, that surely this man has been with Jesus of Nazareth, since even his speech betrays him? (Matthew xxvi, 73)

When an author issues such a sweeping and entirely undocumented indictment of religious community life as to say that when we sing the familiar psalm, "O how good and how pleasant it is for brethren to dwell together in unity," hundreds of nuns *he* knows will reply, "Fooey!" it might be well to pursue his point and discover that these same nuns are very probably the cause for any "fooeyness" in their own communities. While many a religious will accept the stinging indictments of this kind of writing in silence or even praise its good intention, which we do not question here, it should be fairly obvious to anyone, priest or nun, who has had even limited experience of religious life, that the religious of the "fooey" reaction are not exactly the cream of their communities.

For all religious, as for all mankind, there is suffering to be borne. It can happen that spectacular suffering may come to a religious from an exceptionally bad community situation. It does regularly happen that unspectacular sufferings turn up. Once St. Colette was asked by her nuns what she considered the greatest misfortune that could befall her. The saint replied: "To pass a day without suffering something for God." Colette would have given the house psychiatrist rather a jolt with that reply, had her monastery engaged one.

What is so striking—and, yes, so frightening—in scores of articles on the causes of defection from religious life is that loss of the spirit of prayer is never mentioned. It is explained to us that just as girls do not enter the convent because they do not like the cut of the Habit, so professed religious leave because they are misunderstood, rejected, overlooked, wrongly blamed, asked to submit instead of being engaged in a dialogue with the superior, etc., etc. Yet, there has never been a case where a true vocation was lost unless the spirit of prayer was first lost. Let the most understood, accepted, praised, honored, and trusted religious give up prayer, and we shall see what has become of her in just a few weeks.

Why, instead of flailing out against the structure of religious life, do we not urge suffering religious to become more deeply prayerful religious in crisis? "And being in an agony, He prayed the longer." (Luke xxii,43) An unfortunate community situation or an evil-tongued companion can cause great anguish to a religious. So can interior problems. St. Paul had his share of both. And God's answer to Paul is God's answer to any religious who thinks this thing is too big for her: "My grace is sufficient for thee." (2 Cor. xx,9)

This is not to say that superiors can do no wrong or that they should not consistently strive to become better superiors, any more than it is to maintain that troublemaking religious are the salt of the earth and need not be checked. But it is to maintain that the *root* of defections from religious life is defection from prayer. How determinedly we can kick against the goad just when God is striving for our perfection.

When we are convinced that extraordinary suffering is intolerable, it will not be too long before we come to believe that small sufferings, too, must be shaken off. By that time we shall have abandoned clear thinking and thrown in our cause with the neurotic god so that normal joys as well as normal sorrows will be regarded with hostility and aversion. We shall resent anything or anyone who tries us, and we shall leave off simple, gay recreations in favor of contrived ones.

Why must we suspect naturalness, normalcy, and above all, happiness in religious life? In the torrents of words pouring out about how nuns' recreations should be conducted, the villain in the piece seems to be that "big table." And when the neurotic god comes to recreation in the cloister (a thing he abhors doing, but which is necessary for the compilation of his case histories' file), he will see in action what he and some current writers have discussed at length. A group of adult women sit about that "big table" which so affronts the literary liberators, talking a little sober sense and a lot of frank nonsense, darning mantles, folding greeting cards. And a determined soul at the end of the table sorts out Betty Crocker coupons, remarking with satisfaction that we need only two thousand more to get a new double-boiler for the kitchen. Before all the crusaders fall upon this assembly with outraged cries at how intelligence is being stultified, freedom shackled, and the cultural level held at its lowest point, we may need to clarify a few matters. What is the purpose of community recreation? What is its particular function in a cloister?

By evening, a tired teaching Sister who has lectured, answered questions, posed problems all day in a classroom will obviously need a different kind of recreation than does the tired cloistered nun who has kept conversational silence all day, chanted the Divine Office, and done her share of silent manual and mental labor. The professional problems of the former or that day's new educational challenges in the classroom could perhaps well be discussed with other experienced religious in the community to the relaxation and common advantage of all. Or perhaps not. Maybe a tired teacher would simply like to relax in silence or put some good records on the community record-player, along with a group of like-minded Sisters. Again, maybe a short session of intimate family nonsense is exactly what she needs. And a wise superior will certainly allow a fitting freedom for such Sisters. In a cloister, the set-up is different.

The writers who urge that religious should devote their recreation to serious discussions of professional problems may or may not be right as concerns teachers or nurses. They are decidedly wrong as concerns contemplatives. At our federal chapters, the professional concerns of our cloistered life are discussed. It is very helpful. It is educational. It is needful. The fact that the capitulars are exhausted by the end of a day's sessions shows how recreational it is.

Precisely because her life is dedicated exclusively to the

spiritual, the contemplative nun's recreation must prescind from the exclusively spiritual. A higher spiritual and intellectual level in a cloister is never less achieved than when recreations in a cloister are devoted to discussions of the spiritual life and when unabashed gaiety is held suspect. St. Teresa of Avila once discovered a group of her nuns praying the rosary at recreation, instead of talking together. She did not praise them for devoting their recreation period to the things of the spirit. She told them very tartly that women are sufficiently foolish by nature without trying to become more foolish by grace. And while it is true that the case of praying the rosary is not the same as the case of discussing the rosary, the point is still valid.

It was Teresa who snatched up the figure of the Christ-Child from the crib and danced around the community room with it in her arms, Teresa who made up little rhymes and songs to entertain her daughters, Teresa who played the castanets and laughed so much and so easily. It was the same with Clare of Assisi who was so gay in the Lord that she said she "found no suffering too hard, no penance too difficult, no illness too burdensome." It was the great contemplative Clare who kept a little cat which she alternately scolded and petted and which managed to get itself involved in the process of her canonization. And it was Clare whom Daniel-Rops declares was not less a great mystic when she amused herself at recreation with her Sisters than when she was at prayer. Amused herself, remember, not refreshed herself with professional discussions.

Roundtable discussions on matters lying at the heart of the contemplative vocation are being held in many monasteries. They are very profitable when properly conducted. But recreation is not the time for these planned discussions.

Discussions of serious matters do often arise at a cloister recreation; and when they do, it is interesting and educational and also recreational in the truest sense of that word to exchange points of view very informally, to get new insights from one another, to discover fresh angles on sundry points. But such discussions must *arise* if they are to be recreational. They cannot be contrived. Spontaneity lies at the heart of any successful and availing recreation.

If it has been a particularly arduous day as concerns physical work, it is unlikely that a serious discussion will arise. Nonsense—good, happy, old-fashioned nonsense—is what is called for. It is what invariably holds sway on such an evening. When we were building our refectory (an euphemistic expression for sacrificing our community room and giving over a storeroom so that they could be converted into a large refectory by the simple expedient of tearing down the wall between them), we were wearier than usual by evening. The portresses had been escorting plumbers, electricians, and bricklayers up and down the stairs as a daylong occupation. How little we had dreamed that "just tearing down a wall" involved so much of wires, gas, water, chimney soot, and falling plaster! The young nuns had been steering mops across floors traced in surrealistic patterns of black chimney soot. Everyone was disconnected and uncoordinated. It was scarcely the time to discuss the dark night of the soul. It was exactly the time to laugh over foolish family jokes, to tease, to have conducted tours of the big, ugly, dirty shell which was going to become our beautiful, sunlit refectory. So that is what we did. We did not need assorted diversions or contrived relaxation. We did not need anything except one another. And that, thank God, is what we always have.

Availing recreations unfailingly shape themselves, sometimes foolish, sometimes serious, usually a mixture of both. Any contemplative who has persevered into middle years in the cloister will certainly understand that nonsense is increasingly necessary at recreation *according as* the life is lived with sober sense.

A nun obliged to continual silence all day is going to find one hour of free conversation with her companions a perfectly delightful, wholly satisfying thing. Of course, if she has not fulfilled her obligation and has been talking a good part of the day, then obviously talking at recreation will not be a refreshing or diverting experience. Such a person will have to look for other diversions, and her relaxation will need to be contrived. The contemplative life without its recreational soupçon of nonsense would be insupportable. To make its recreation "professional" would only be to endanger its proper functioning outside recreation.

The purpose of recreation in a religious community is the same as that of any genuine recreation: to re-create, that is, to refresh and renew the powers of mind and body for a return to duty. The contemplative will have to do this in a different way from others, since her particular kind of professional duty is indeed particularized. And so the neurotic god needs to stand back and take a second look at these "boring, fettered recreations" around that formidable "big table" so as to get a different perspective. The only trouble is that he never will. He came to recreation with his preconceived ideas. He departs early and gets back to his case histories, so as not to run any danger of changing his ideas.

While the neurotic god is squinting nervously at nuns around the big table, he ought to make a point of listening, too. For, if patching aprons and talking is such a deadly business, why are the nuns obviously having such a wonderful time? And if their mental horizons are persistently dwindling, how is it that they find such riches in one another?

In the book written after his tour of Russia, Adlai Stevenson contrasted the channelling of Russian energies and talent with the American "frittering away of talent, time, and resources on trivialities." Whatever we may think of Russia's channelling methods, directions taken, and calibre of ideals, we must honestly wince at the "trivialities"—that is, if we are still capable of defining trivialities. In fact, we might venture to amend Mr. Stevenson's statement that we fritter away our talent, time, and resources on what we do not recognize as trivialities.

A contemplative nun fritters away her talent, time, and resources on trivialities when she talks all day in the name of "outgoing charity." She renews her resources, shares her talents for increasing communal joy, and demonstrates that she has not frittered away her time during the silent day when she is gay and talkative and completely spontaneous at recreation. Where did we get this trivial idea that outgoing means no indwelling? Contemplative silence, like contemplative prayer, is thoroughly outgoing. It has meaning for all the world. The personal sanctification of the cloistered religious is the most outgoing contribution she can make to society. The contemplative who is garrulous outside recreation is not so much outgoing as merely outgushing. A necklace of bangles is just as effective a halter for hanging ourselves as a rope. And the neurotic god's theses are all necklaces of bangles.

While he is insisting that a nun's personality is going to break out in measles if she does not escape the close air of stultified recreational conversations, the nun herself may be consistently learning a great deal from these same conversations. It was amusing to overhear an elderly nun discussing with a slightly younger nun at recreation the meaning of this mysterious phrase "rock 'n roll" which they had come across in an article on music. The slightly-less-aged nun was frankly at a loss. She could not hazard a guess. Then the older gave it as her opinion that it had something to do with the listing of a ship. She volunteered a technical explanation of the roll of a ship, how it is measured, what it affects, until her companion was satisfied that rock 'n roll was a matter peculiar to the listing of seagoing vessels.

Yet, this quaint etymologist was the same one who was troubled a few evenings later at another recreation over an historical book we were reading. The author's logic was spurious, she complained. And she proceeded to unthread the man's false subtleties with a deftness many a professional philosopher could envy. This old nun could have quite a lot to say about what is trivial, and under what circumstances, and what is important and when.

The neurotic god beats his fists in protest at the "big table" where nuns who are silent all day, and striving to be prayerful and penitential all day, often talk recreational nonsense for an hour. When he goes off to take another tranquillizer, these incorrigibly happy case studies of his go off to pray, to paint, to sweep, to analyze, to dig, to suffer, to obey. So, if they want to have a picnic once a year to which he will not come save as a fringe observer, and if they like to sit around a big table nearly every evening of the year, someone should counsel the neurotic god not to get so upset about it. He might get neurotic, worrying so much.

Let us not do the work of the neurotic god for him and create problems where they do not exist. There is no need to torture the perfectly normal, happy functioning of religious life into a pretzel of misery. Spontaneity must be the wellspring of any operative and productive recreation. So if nuns love their big table and those who sit thereat, there seems no particular need to liberate them into contrived recreations. We do not come to the cloister to have a good time. That is part of the reason why we have so many good times. It is not a case of nuns loving the whimsical interchanges of recreation only because they don't know any better, but because they could not want anything better. It should be fairly obvious that all will not be equally charmed with the interests of another. Yet it is scarcely the spiritual adult who proposes solving this minor problem by chipping the community up into similar-interests groups. This is the modus operandi of the hobbies' club, not of the religious community, where it should be understood that the small mortifications inevitable in group recreations are the spiritual preserving salt of them, not a corroding acid. False emphasis on neurosis hazards is often laid by reason of underemphasis on healthy mortification and healthful nonsense as well.

The Poor Clares in Roswell lately became the slightly bewildered possessors of a refrigerator that does not refrigerate. Its viscera are missing. And, to judge by its venerable appearance, it is the original Model-T refrigerator. However, an icebox which does not ice did not prove useless to us. It now stands proudly on the side porch, and it holds our wooden garden sandals. Out of respect for her position, Reverend Mother Abbess was given the freezer compartment. Racks intended for ice cubes hold her garden gloves and marigold seeds. Anti-mosquito squirt remains unfrozen and accessible in the freezer.

We find it impressive to have an icebox for a sandal cupboard. The plumber found it impressive, too, when he was enlisted to lend a muscle to the two kind men coaxing the imposing old icebox up the porch stairs, and being urged by Sister Paschal to "put it two inches that way please; and another inch back,—no it's not straight. It won't look neat. Ah, there!"

"You keep your icebox on the porch?" the plumber asked uncertainly. "Yes," said Sister Paschal, beaming. "We keep our garden shoes in it." His face was, as we say, a study. But when the matter was explained to him, the plumber rallied to our way of thinking. It was only as he was going down the stairs, however, that the full impact got him. He clung weakly to the bannister in his enjoyment. "Keep their shoes in the icebox," he chuckled. "Hey, that's pretty good."

But what does the neurotic god think of the silly thing, I wonder?

11

The Convex God at Home

The convex god and his doctrine of push-away has enlarged his cult quite alarmingly in past years. He has so much to further his cause: our speed, our wholesale production of everything including thoughts and opinions, our consciousness of teetering on the edge of nuclear destruction. There is not time or space enough for giving personal love a chance to reach the luxuriant growth of which it is always capable. He even has high-sounding if false spirituality on his side, this ugly little convex god. The touch-me-not sign he prints across creatures and creation reads smoothly enough. His success is apparent in a Christian too busy to love. His triumph is a religious so determined to "perfect" herself that she has no time or sense left for giving herself.

Back in the dim ages when some of us saw films, there was being foisted on the public a film about cloistered nuns. A certain reel showed the nuns kneeling at Mass. One toppled over in a faint. Did the others rush to her side and pick her up? Indeed not. They belonged to the convex cult. They were too intent on their devotions to be devoted. The odd thing about this sequence was that the film was not condemning the nuns. It was admiringly picturing their recollection and detachment. The same kind of nonsense has appeared more recently in a best-selling novel about nuns. It is worth mentioning only because it is a highly exaggerated symbol of false detachment, hollow "perfection," and false and hollow womanhood. Because it is so exaggerated, it may help us see the point a little faster.

What do we mean by detachment? And what is the evil of attachment? By reason of her close-range living with companions who are probably not going to be sent to another parish, diocese, or province this side of eternity, a cloistered nun may be equipped to make a few valid observations on these points. If she is attached to her sisters in religion, it will not be the result of having glamorized them. It cannot be. They are there, right there, all the time, in their best moments and in their worst. She will have to love them—warts, wrinkles and all, or not at all. And that is the way they will have to love her or not love her. The effort to love or the decision not to love in a contemplative community is definitely not going to be based on retouched photographs but on poor, battered old human nature as it is.

Whereas it should be made clear to young religious that affectionate attachment to her companions is the triumph of charity, the point is sometimes left quite obscure while she is warned about particular friendships, cliques, and selectiveness. In truth, these are formidable threats to the Christlike love which should be palpable in a religious community; but, like "emotional disturbances," these terms have another meaning besides the ugly technical one,—a beautiful, natural meaning. Many a young religious has suffered bewilderment and misery because the non-technical meaning was not sorted out for her.

Friendship by its very nature is particular. We may feel benevolent toward humanity in general, but we love a friend very much in particular. To be a friend to someone is immediately to be a very particular person to her. To aspire to have a particular holy friendship with each member of the community should be the goal of a religious. It is the duty of a superior. It seems a great pity that what divides, destroys, debauches, and in its final stage perverts, should ever have been honored with the title of friendship. That which is the enemy of everything wholesome and normal in community life is also the particular enemy of those who indulge it. Particular friendship in the technical sense would have been better named Specialized Uncharity.

Similarly, if cliques can be and are sometimes formed in a community to the inevitable breaking down of communal love, there is another and very happy sense in which the community itself is a clique, a small group of persons united in a common cause, diverted from the general course of things for a specialized end. Once when we had read an article that issued especially stern warnings against cliques in community life, someone remarked glumly at recreation that the trouble with trying to start a clique in our community is that everyone would immediately join it. It has become legendary here that the only way a nun can be absolutely sure of a full house at recreation when she wishes to say something is to turn to one Sister and begin talking in a whisper. Everyone else is at once interested and alert. And amid the inevitable laughter, the whisperer gets and holds the floor, at least for a while. It has been done so often that it is remarkable how it still never fails. Just give any indication of a clique, and the nuns line up to join it, twenty strong.

As for selectiveness, a woman selected by God to be His spouse has entered a selective group to do selective work. She has been selective all the way down the line, and especially so in electing to lavish her love on this particular little group of people so that her love may radiate out into the world through them. And lavish *is* the word. Love is not something to be preserved in the alcohol of false detachment, but to be poured out. The pouring out is the very means of increase. Just as Christ warned us that we shall lose our life in the measure we strive to keep it, so we may need to recall that the surest way to lose love, even the very power to love, is to keep it.

How many pens have driven across how many pages to warn religious and all serious Christians of the dangers of attachments! The spectacle of a hurrying, "detached" humanity which is sometimes singularly inhumane may alone prompt us to wonder whether there is not something to be said on the side of attachment. From the sharp elbowers on the subway to the religious encircled by her private concerns, there would seem to be a possibility that a little more attachment to our fellows might not be too bad a thing.

But before the ghosts of some nineteenth-century spiritual writers rise up to besiege us, we had better hasten to define our position with a question: Is "harmful attachments" a valid term to apply to human love? Or is it not true that there is only one injurious attachment which spawns a thousand ugly, grasping little reptiles? The testimony of the cloister where fraternal living is too compressed for glossing is that harmful attachment does not have a plural but only a progeny.

Either you are attached to yourself, or you are not (by which latter is meant that you are striving to become unattached, since the final and complete separation will be witnessed only in eternity, human nature being what it is). And as love is woman's destiny, and particularized love the special field of religious women, it follows that a nun's work is to get progressively unattached to herself. For only then will she be free enough to get attached to anything and anyone else, since detachment from self leads us into that large, free country of God's own very attached love for His creatures. We tend to think of attachments as fetters, whereas fetters are actually part only of the single attachment which is attachment to self. Just as there is no one so coldly detached from others as the person deeply attached to herself, so only the soul detached from absorption with herself is free enough and capacious enough to take the interests of others into the warm embrace of her love and the attachment of her vital interest.

God's determination to love man despite man's failures, betrayals, and rejections of divine love is something unfathomable before which we can only marvel perpetually. He simply will not break off relations with a soul. Even when a soul breaks off relations with Him, He goes on pursuing it with an attachment that would have to be infinite. God will detach Himself from a creature only at the ultimate rejection by the creature, which is death in sin and consequent damnation. Yet, even hell and its agonies cry out the attachment of God to His creatures, the attachment they consistently refused and which they will eternally proclaim by the wrenchings and groanings of their elected separation from Him. A creature who would hold other creatures at arm's length will have to find another model for his behavior than his Creator. The convex god will serve him well.

St. Francis prayed to be "detached from all things under heaven." That what he meant by detachment is something entirely different from the anemic concepts some of us may have in that regard is immediately testified by his own life. It is difficult to summon the image of a saint more in love with beauty, life, song, and human beings than detached Francis. He had room in his seraphic heart for every beggar, leper and outcast, every prince and cardinal and king. Those were no ersatz tears he wept for his errant sons. There was no puritanical distrust of nature's charms in his song to Brother Sun when his eyes were tortured and nearly blind.

Francis, who begged pardon of his own dying body for the hard treatment he had given it through life, had got detached from himself rather more thoroughly than most men do and rather beyond what most men ambition. His prayer to be detached from all things under heaven clearly meant those things which would not be one day taken with him into heaven but were meant to remain "under heaven." It was because he accomplished the tremendous spiritual feat of stepping out of self-love that Francis was so gloriously free to love other persons. His prayer was answered when, detached from himself, he could happily attach himself to every soul fortunate enough to cross his path. No one will argue that the generations of more than seven centuries since his death have not shown an extraordinary attachment in return to the little friar who loved men so deeply.

St. Augustine's famous dictum, "Love God, and do what you will," is less the pretty bit of poetry some quote it as being than an acute and extremely demanding regimen for the soul. It may seem a charming saying. Actually, it is a very hard saying, and not many can take it. St. Francis' life was a certain paraphrase of Augustine's word. It read: "Be detached from yourself, and you may then attach yourself to every soul whose destiny is heaven." This is, in fact, what lies at the heart of the contemplative vocation of his daughters, and what was so manifest in the first of his daughters, Clare.

When the tentacles of our nature close in about itself, we become the omnivorous animal, and every object of our "affection" is someone or something to be devoured. This is the attachment against which we must certainly take precautions. It is insidious and in the end utterly destructive of charity. But the insidiousness of attachment is a matter of direction. It is evil when it turns in upon self. It is wonderfully, beautifully good when it turns outward from a self-detached heart and gathers the concerns of others into the arms of its warm compassion and love. This is the true outgoing charity.

Because St. Francis and St. Clare had shaken free of any self-attachment, they could afford to be attached to everyone else. And so they had no false need to push the world away, to hold their companions at a good safe distance, to lead a convex life.

When Clare and her sister, Agnes, were separated for many years, they exchanged some remarkably undetached letters. "I find no consolation, no matter where I seek it," wrote St. Agnes, frankly admitting she had tried a number of emotional spas and found them wanting. "I feel grief upon grief when I think I can never expect to see you again." And Clare writes to Blessed Agnes of Prague that hearing of the latter's health and happiness and spiritual progress had quite overwhelmed her with joy and gladness. Another time in a rush of affection, Clare calls Agnes "half of my soul," and "the shrine of my heart's special love." When the dead body of St. Francis was brought to the grille of her monastery along the way of the funeral procession, however much she rejoiced in his glory, Clare still wept aloud at the earthly parting from him, kissed his wounded feet, and pressed little pieces of linen against the sacred stigmata to comfort her heart and her daughters in the lonely days ahead. Such holy and blessed attachments are possible only to the soul so detached from itself that a convex philosophy about others is the remotest of all heresies.

In the Office of St. Clare's feast on August 12, Holy Church joyously reminds us in one of the antiphons that Pope Gregory loved her as a father. Obviously, Clare loved him as a daughter. Into a life of austerity, St. Clare breathed inexhaustible love. Her affection embraced every living creature in her monastery from her Sisters to her kitten. And she frankly hoped to be loved in return. "Always bear love to me," she wrote in her last testament to her spiritual daughters. Her final command to them was a word of love: "Let the love which you have in your hearts be shown outwardly by your deeds." Clare was never an uninterested, detached spectator of community life. We cannot picture to ourselves an uninterested Christ. And Clare strove to love as He loved. Her success is attested by the Church in the very first antiphon of her Vespers for August 12: "The brightness of Clare has filled the whole world." There is only one light bright enough to illuminate the whole world. Love.

The convex god advocates perfection. He promises its attainment by a neat self-absorption—that is, by so comprehensive an attachment to one's self that there is no question of anything but a prophylactic relation with anyone else; that cold withdrawal from others which has masqueraded often enough as "detachment." Such a relationship can, of course, be turned inside out, in which case it appears not as a withdrawal but as a consuming affection for others. But it is the same self-attachment, right side or inside out. And there is the same basic false detachment from others, for we are equally uninterested in the true welfare of others whether we ignore them or devour them.

God has placed tremendous riches of tenderness in the heart of any normal woman. Turned outward on souls, there is little to surpass this tenderness of womanly love in power to achieve good. Turned inward upon self, however, it becomes that ugly absorption which is the only harmful attachment there is. We come to religious life unattached to one another, strangers. And many a spiritual book pleads with us to practise more and more detachment from creatures. Yet, all the time, what we need most is detachment from one creature only. We shall always happily return to the same point of truth if only we refuse to commit our thinking to the convex god; we shall continually see that all these so-called attachments to creatures reduce to an attachment to oneself. When we love anyone possessively, we are merely exercising our acquisitive instincts. We want someone's affection, attention, admiration. It is possible to spend a lifetime indulging oneself, attached to oneself, in the name of a great love for others, just as it is possible to waste a lifetime in backing away from others and simultaneously retreating more deeply into self-interest.

True enough, spiritual love as well as carnal love seeks of its nature to possess the beloved. Yet, this is not to devour. Two in one flesh, but still two. Twenty in one cloister, remaining twenty in their spiritual unity of Christlike love. Two in the secret of prayer, yet still one God and one creature, however identified in moments of true mystical union. The same kind of self-aggrandizement by which we may seek to direct the opinions, the views, even the whole lives of others, informs the "prayer" which seeks to bend God to its wish rather than to bend itself to God's Will. All this is the work of the convex god who is anxious that we should not understand how a devouring false attachment to others is actually a perfect detachment from their true good. He is just as anxious to convince us that we must push the world away to be perfect within. There are assorted methods for living a convex life, and the convex god is expert in adaptation. He suits his method and adjusts his doctrine to the temperament of each prospective convert.

St. Teresa of Avila, quite as frankly as St. Clare, admitted her affectionate attachment to her daughters, remarking that although she was detached from many things, she was not at all detached from her Sisters, and adding with some satisfaction that she thought they were attached to her, too. We are so diligently warned against loving too much. Why are we not warned against the only real failure there is: loving too little? Rushing our way through life as we pant on toward perfection, we may trip over the souls in our paths, only to gather our forces and make another forward sprint, instead of stopping, stooping, and loving. As we all so desperately need to be stooped to, so do we need sometimes to stoop. We who require constant lifting may be also required at times to lift.

Reticence has retired from the pages of a number of our modern religious books and journals to the extent that excesses and perversions which formerly many young religious never knew existed are now clearly labelled, analyzed, dissected, and the parts paraded. If warmed-over Victorianism is an unhealthy approach to religious instruction, it can scarcely be called wholesome, either, to present perversions as quite run-of-the-mill. It is possible to get so clinical in our presentation of chastity that the good smell of lavender is rubbed off love and friendship.

If we encourage our young religious to love rightly, our

pens will not need to be quite so busy in warning them not to love wrongly. One image of true and holy friendship, of sincere and blessed outgoing attachment, is more effective for good than a hundred cautionary clinical observations and dark detailed examples of unwholesome relationships. We can grow so intent on studying thorns as to forget we really started out to talk about roses. The convex god does not much believe in roses. Or, if he does, he cannot see them for the thorns.

When we experiment with living a push-away life as concerns our immediate companions in the community, it becomes easy to grow convex also about the even more immediate companions of our existence: our own sorrows and joys. We can with alarming facility accept the thesis of the convex god that suffering is a thing to be held at arm's length, to be combatted, to be driven from the field. The effort to clear our private arena of its lions can preoccupy us to the extent that we have not a moment to reflect that perhaps God wants those particular lions to devour us, that so we may enter into our glory which is His glory.

It is a basic instinct of human nature to ward off pain. Even our reflex actions support this line of procedure. When we are falling, we throw out our own protective arms. When a foreign particle hurls itself at our eye, we close our eye. If it does get in, we try to blink it out. This is all very good, physically speaking, but not equally good spiritually speaking. We can waste a great deal of spiritual energy living convexly, assiduously pushing away the very sufferings which God has intended should become part of our spiritual fabric and be our strength. That is why God must sometimes save us from our own stagnation by sending us suffering we cannot push away, which will render us concave by the very force of its impact.

By consistently trying to clear our path of the small sufferings which we may have come to regard as rubble on the way, we can even come to accept the word of the convex god that we are actually suffering well. We are keeping life tidy. We are faithfully trying to push away every annoyance, every irritation, every intrusion on our plans. But to fancy one is suffering well is the final delusion. And perhaps that is why, when we seem to have got a settled false perspective on pain, God rescues us with His truth by means of some smashing, shattering sorrow that leaves the soul reeling. The comfortable routine of push-away is forcibly snatched from us, and the protesting, frightened heart is alone.

The mystery of suffering closes its darkness around us, and we are prostrated by this one unimaginable thing. For the sufferings that rip open the seams of the soul and leave us more concave to grace are always the unthinkable, unimaginable ones, never those that figured in our portrait of perfection. Thus and so it may possibly be, this ogre or that phantom may assault me, but there are out-of-orbit spectres which can never reach my particular planet. Then the moment comes, untrumpeted and even sometimes unrumored. And the defenses of years are levelled in an instant. Our practised combats, our fellowship with mortification, our custombuilt garment of patience,—what are these frail defenses before the terror of the unlooked-for blow?

And so we are stripped of the aristocracy of elected penance. No one is tempted to feel spiritually refined when he is cringing on the ground before suffering, when his full effort would be concentrated at warding it off if it were not quite impossible even to attempt any convex action. Perhaps the only extrinsic reality of which such a sufferer remains aware is that his privacy, too, has been violated. When grief is sufficiently fierce, it can no more be hidden than any other roaring lion, at least certainly not in the little compound of religious community life. So it announces itself to all. And we crouch back against the pain, ashamed at its publication, with no hiding-place.

This is the hour of God's tenderest mercy. For this is when we have to bow our heads and see what all must see: our pitiable smallness, our revolt, our wild but very human protest at the violation of our complacency. At such moments we see there is nothing left in us of the strength we were deluded into thinking we had. We can only cast ourselves with a great cry into the arms of God. This is perhaps the beginning of humility, whose contours are never convex.

To take our sorrows into our own lives is not a matter of endurance. We can endure out of necessity while the whole force of our desire pushes the suffering away. To enter into a suffering and let the suffering enter into us is a matter of acceptance. And acceptance is what ripens and perfects. It is only when the seed dies that it brings forth much fruit, our patient God has pointed out to us.

It has been so well said that the great classic tragedies of drama leave us feeling cleansed and fortified, not weakened or depressed. This applies very exactly to the world of the spirit, to the personal tragedies within. But if they are to cleanse and to strengthen us, they must be within,—tragedies consciously taken into self and woven like strong thread into the fabric of the spirit.

Suffering never happens to us, any more than the companions of our life just happened to be dropped down beside us in the community. Suffering is planned. The companions were planned. If only it were not so sad, what a droll picture that would be of the little convex heretic in the middle of his private arena, energetically fisting away the sanctifying sorrow, determinedly holding at arm's length the shapers of his glory.

Holy Church repeatedly encourages us to pray for unending joy. Yet not to take the sufferings of life into the arms of our being is to be left unprepared for joy, uncleansed for it. Nothing occurs in our lives without significance, but it is easy enough for us to miss the significance. The convex god is so eager to help us miss it.

Having rejected suffering, it follows logically that we shall be suspicious of authentic joy. When sorrow has not ploughed up our souls, they are not ready to receive the seeds of gladness. Thus we discover the convex god's followers holding off the joys of life as well as its sufferings. St. Francis seems never to have missed a joy in all his life. He improvised a fiddle out of two sticks, he sang for the sheer joy of having a Father in heaven, he relished Lady Giacoma's little almond cakes, and he would have had fiddling and song when he was dying save that some of his more convex sons feared the neighbors might be disedified if the blind and pain-racked saint should die so gaily. Yet this same exuberant Francis was moved to curse his false sons who strove to tear down what his true sons built up. He grieved passionately over the watering down of his ideal. And the five wounds with which Christ marked his frail body were for Francis' torture as much as for our joy. Suffering and joy, joy and suffering; Francis took them to his heart just as he took everyone he met into his heart. He was not the man to hold his nose against the fragrance of a rose or to put on dark glasses when the lilacs bloomed. He was a fugitive neither from his own sorrows and joys nor from the needs of his fellows. He was and remains the despair of the convex god. It is the particular business of his followers to be hammerers at the heresy of the convex god.

There is a great deal being written about people who have been made to feel rejected. Maybe more needs to be written about the rejectors. They are in a far worse predicament, however little they suspect it.

When St. Clare in her rule posts a "Beware!" sign on such matters as envy, detraction, murmuring, vainglory and their dreary company, and when she appoints the penance for a contemptuous nun to perform, it is evident that she had met in religion some of humanity's more inglorious specimens and was not merely jotting down a few theoretical possibilities that had occurred to her at her knitting. She had accepted the weakness and perhaps occasionally the malice of others and had let it exercise its appointed work on her own life. She was not so tender, so gay, so loving an abbess and mother because she had kept her own life detachedly pleasant by warding off the needs or the unpleasantness of others, but precisely because she had gathered her monastic family so closely to her heart.

St. Francis detested lepers, until the day he kissed one. In the end, the only way we can discover the lovableness of those around us is to love them. And the only time we can fail to learn great lessons from our companions is when we hold them at arm's length in that convex detachment which is the most self-righteous form of self-attachment.

The convex god deals exclusively in negatives. Fend off our fellows, ward off our woes, suspect our joys. And all the time it is the love of our companions and the acceptance of both sufferings and gladness that make spiritual sinew. The push-away doctrine of the convex god denies any personal meaning for us in our circumstances, situation, or companions. It is bad enough to make the mistake of listening to his heresy. It is far worse to serve it up to our young religious as though it were wholesome food. The most natural posture of motherhood is that of the arms held out and curved to hold and to love. The most truly supernatural interior posture of consecrated virginity is of spiritual arms held out and curved to hold and to love. The religious woman, the virgin, is a bride. She is the bride of Christ, the Head of the human race. Cold, uninterested "detachment" from the humanity her Spouse has loved unto death, and an absorbing attachment to herself are scarcely the spiritual garments befitting such a bride. The garb is even less becoming when worn in the midst of His very own, her very own: her community.

On August 12, we sing the Transitus of St. Clare, the commemoration of her death. Part of this thoroughly joyous marking of her deathday is the singing of her last words: "Go in peace, my blessed soul!" Clare loved her own soul tenderly, and that was the way she loved others. She was an expert in particular friendships in the healthy and holy sense of the term. And she knew her soul was blessed, just as she had proceeded all through life on the assumption that the souls of her companions were blessed and very well worth the particular loving. Her words of encouragement to her own soul about to break free of her suffering body express the core of her spirituality and her philosophy: "You will have the best of companions on your journey, my soul: He who made you and sanctified you and has loved you as a mother loves her child." That was the way Clare loved. It is the way a religious is destined by God to love. There has never been a convex-minded mother, except the caricatures of motherhood.

We sing the *Transitus* at sunset when the August evening is settling over the monastery. The sweet-smelling melons lie roundly in the field. Pink Japanese lilies fleck the flowerbeds. The trees and lawns and bushes have reached the fulfilment of themselves. It is an hour to hold to the heart. It is not at all a proper setting for the sworn enemy of fulfilment, the convex god. "As a mother loves her child," we sing a second time. And then because love has been recognized as the only apostolate having significance before God, we cry out in a final antiphon: "Clare, spouse of God, lead us to the realms of the stars!"

12

The Convex God Abroad

"O my God, I offer Thee this spiritual reading. Grant that it may be for Thy greater honor and glory and the salvation of souls." Before the beginning of common work, nuns pray together. When the bell summons them to recreation, they pray together before they begin to laugh together. When the rising bell ends their sleep, even as they raise heavy eyelids and test the locomotive powers of sleep-wobbly limbs, they are praying that they "may rise to a new life and be entirely united to You, my God." It is all very impressive as well as confusing to a new postulant. But I found particularly impressive the little prayer offered to God before spiritual reading.

In the more personal pursuits in religious life, a nun's private spiritual reading might be expected to occur high on the list. If she works for the common good, prays for the Church, and does penance for sinners, at least when she sits down with a book of ascetical principles, mystical theology, or hagiography she is engaged in a strictly personal activity. She is enlarging her knowledge, deepening her faith and understanding, activating her devotedness. It is her business. Her soul. Her choice of book. Her conclusions. Yet the ancient monastic prayer beseeches God that the reading may avail for the salvation of souls. How can it? What does the personal sanctification of one nun in one obscure cloister have to do with anyone's soul but her own?

The answer lies at the very heart of the contemplative life. The personal sanctification of the contemplative *is* her work for the salvation of souls. She will be the "co-worker with Christ" which St. Clare insisted she must be in the exact measure that she strives to be holy. Again, in the measure that she fails to attain to that profound union with God which is her hidden vocation in the Church, in that same measure she fails the Church and society. And so the postulant is given to understand from the beginning of her contemplative life that every detail of her vocation involves the world. Even her spiritual reading must avail for souls if it is to avail for herself.

A considerable amount of writing is being done to warn religious of the fallacy of centering attention on the matter of personal sanctification instead of the matter of service. It is certainly true that the dark triumph of convexism is a preoccupation with personal sanctification to the extent that service is bypassed or at least reduced to a low level of importance. However, this would be an affair of falsification rather than of overemphasis. For, as a matter of fact, entire preoccupation with self precludes personal sanctification. Goodness is diffusive of itself. Any Christian who seeks personal identification with Christ by pushing other Christians away is a dubious Christian. The religious who does this is the true neurotic, since neuroticism is a partial withdrawal from reality. She may even be, in this sense, a species of psychotic. Convexism practised to its perfection would become a synonym for psychosis, the full withdrawal from reality. For the reality of the Christian vocation is outgoing love.

However, to imply that personal sanctification should or even can be put aside in favor of service is to have pulled so strenuously at one false idea as to have fallen over backwards and to have landed, judging by some of the remarkable statements issuing from this kind of reasoning, on the back of one's head. It is simply not reasonable for a religious to discard silence, private prayer, spiritual reading, and the practice of recollection in the name of service. A vacuum and a horn of plenty are two quite different things. To think we can be a channel when we have never been a reservoir is to be the very wildest knight who ever journeyed along singing a song in search of an El Dorado.

While it is true to say that a line of distinction must not be drawn between perfection of oneself and service of one's neighbor, still it is false to hold that looking first to one's own sanctification is to fail to look to the salvation of others. What has somehow got buried under a great mound of words is the unchangeable truth that genuine personal sanctification is of itself service supreme to others. If we do not believe this, we do not understand the doctrine of the Mystical Body of Christ, or else we do not accept it. Personal holiness necessarily includes holding the world in one's arms. For to be holy is to be Christ.

The nun who keeps the silence enjoined by her rule when she would like to talk, who mortifies her curiosity, who performs hidden acts of self-denial, is serving society quite as realistically as, and possibly more availingly than, the religious on the Red Cross auxiliary board. It is worth remembering that the popes have declared that a religious who keeps her rule perfectly practises heroic *charity*. In our eagerness to do, we cannot afford to forget our obligation to be. There are many forms of service, but no form of service is spiritually efficacious unless the server has Christ to give. If a religious has only herself to give, she may give brilliantly and extensively as the world judges, but she gives nothing of the spiritually enduring. Thus we need to consider whether in an excess of enthusiasm for activity, we are not inadvertently confounding worldly values with spiritual values.

While it is a service to religious when really thoughtful churchmen point out the evident necessity for active religious of our times to enter more fully into parochial life, it is a disservice to religious and to religion when less profound thinkers belabor this idea into false and superficial conclusions. To say, for example, that a nun can never hope to find God apart from contact with the world is scarcely a sound piece of thinking. This would require not only that we uncanonize all the anchoresses and hermits and every contemplative raised to the altars of the Church (and there is a goodly number of them), but also that we revert, not progress, to the heresy about which the late Father Garrigou-Lagrange observed: "The most serious offense seemed to them [the modernists] to be abstention from social works; consequently the purely contemplative life was considered quite useless or the lot of the incapable. God Himself willed to reply to this objection by the canonization of St. Therese of the Child Jesus and by the extraordinary radiation of that contemplative soul."[1]

This is not to issue an apologetic for the contemplative life. It is only to suggest a need to think a little more calmly and a great deal more profoundly on the ratio between indwelling and outgoing holiness—that is, charity—in any religious

[1] Reginald Garrigou-Lagrange, O.P., *The Three Ages of the Interior Life* (St. Louis, Herder), vol. i, p. 277.

whether active or contemplative. To outgo without consistently and persistently striving to indwell is to chase a phantom ideal of charity. It is a very wise movement in many active congregations of religious at the present time that thirty-day retreats are offered to their religious at intervals of years. It recognizes that to be more outgoing it is first of all necessary to be more indwelling. There must be something of true spirituality worthy to go out, and it must first come in through the Holy Spirit who dwells in the quiet places of the soul and the silence of the heart. No amount of doing will supply for a deficiency in being.

St. Francis of Assisi was certainly a saint of the marketplace. He was also the saint of the hermitage. The *carceri,* those little caves of retirement into which he and his friars "came home" after their preaching and serving and healing, are not so much part of the mystery of his holiness as its explanation. No man was more a man among men than St. Francis. Yet, after the example of the Divine Master, he frequently went off alone to pray. And it was alone, at prayer, on the top of a mountain, that Francis was stigmatized, signed and sealed by the most high God.

To give Christ, it is necessary to strive increasingly to be Christ. This is where mistakes about personal sanctification *versus* outgoing charity are made. There can be no question of "versus." If a religious does not look to her personal sanctification, there is in the sight of God simply nothing in her to outgo, however much she may seem to achieve before men. The convex god understands this only too well and is disturbed at the thought. He prefers that we should not think so deeply as to understand that we never pull souls away from Christ so much as when we suck them into the vacuum of ourselves.

True personal holiness is the most effective means of reaching Christ out to others. The active religious has to proceed in her activities from this basic premise or her activities will be only a little straw. The contemplative religious has to proceed in the hiddenness of her cloistered life from this basic premise or hers will be the most useless life in the world. There is a terrible nakedness in the vocation of the contemplative religious woman. She is not called to do things for others but to live for others. Either she is a person progressively emptying herself of self so that she can take the whole world and its miseries into her heart, or she is not much of anything. Teaching, nursing, social service have their very difficult and demanding aspects, but they are also productive of some tangible results. The contemplative nun's apostolate in the Church is rarely productive of any tangible results. It is not meant to be, for it is a life of pure faith. But this cannot be allowed to incline the contemplative religious toward the convex heresy that she need not involve herself with the needs of the world. On the contrary, she is the one whose vocation calls for the most complete involvement of all. If she does not understand that her life of hidden self-immolation is a holocaust for souls and that her very striving for personal holiness means a gathering of the whole world to her heart, she does not understand her vocation at all. The cloistered contemplative is most a cloistered contemplative when she consciously offers her life in union with Christ for the redemption of many.

After twenty years in the cloister, I find my spine still tingling to the memory of my novice mistress' words to me one September morning a few months after I had entered. Sister Elizabeth had brown eyes, but they looked black that morning with the intensity of her conviction. "Remember," she said, "we don't teach, we don't nurse, we don't go out to convert pagans. We have nothing to justify our existence if we are failures as religious." She fixed that black gaze directly on the center of my soul, it seemed to me, and added: "So, if you are not determined to give God absolutely everything, you will be the biggest sham and failure there ever was." There was a little pause. A fly buzzed. A cricket sang. I thought the fly buzzed: "Sham!" I could hear the cricket singing: "Sham!" And then Sister Elizabeth leaned forward and tapped her left knuckles with her right forefinger. "A husk," she said in a definitive tone, "just a husk, if you live for yourself in the cloister." "A husk," buzzed the fly. "A husk," warned the cricket. I gulped a hard postulant-gulp. "I won't, Dear Mistress," I solemnly swore in an awed whisper. "That's good," came the matter-of-fact reply. "See that you don't," she added, for good measure. And she sent me off to scrub carrots, having helped me to understand that the earnest scrubbing of carrots could avail a great deal for the salvation of souls, just as my spiritual reading was meant to do. Sister Elizabeth had no use at all for the convex god, and every instruction she gave us in the novitiate was a simultaneous flattening of his nose.

Outgoing love must be the thesis of the contemplative nun's lifelong study, for of all possible human anomalies that which should most revolt right reason is a loveless contemplative. Love is her single mission in life, and the very fact that she is where she is and lives in the way that she lives is meant to teach the whole world about the supremacy of God and the supereminence of spiritual values, and *in that way* to minister to every need there is, cutting pathways through the most secret despair and the thickest tangle of sorrow. There is a sense in which the contemplative life has no secondary end as do other states of life. Its primary end, to love God and save souls, is also its secondary end. Its means define its purpose, and its purpose is the only possible explanation of its means. It seeks to serve God only by loving Him, only by being His. It seeks to save souls by loving them in a highly specialized way. And what is there so strong to save as love is?

And so the real work of the contemplative religious is to let God make room in her, hollow her out so that she can hold the world. She has only one particular attachment to abandon, and a limitless number of attachments to take on. The real tragedy in a cloister would be the convex soul, pushing the world away.

As years pass, we make a great discovery. More and more people come into our lives. And there is more and more room in our lives to hold them, not less and less. One does not become bewildered by the myriad problems of numerous persons known to us only by name. Instead, the ache in one's throat for the old lady who is going to be turned out of her home, if God does not intervene quickly, creates a new capacity for suffering with the young father whose wife has died in childbirth. When the old lady writes to the monastery, she knows none of the nuns is going to come running to expostulate with the landlord, nor does she expect a thousand-dollar check in the return letter. The young father is not so unbalanced by grief as to think the nuns will call his wife back to life. What *do* they want? Why do they write?

It is doubtful that the old lady or the young father work out a logical thought pattern on the matter. They reach out by intuition to those whose life business it should be to love them and suffer with them and carry their griefs to God for them when they themselves are inarticulate or afraid. If they send an alms, they expect an alms in return. And the alms they have a right to expect is love. What sustains the old lady is that she is not a case number to be classified and filed, but a person to be individually loved and brooded over in prayer. What clears something of the fog of grief out of the young father's bewildered pain is the fact that loving hands of prayer are held out to him and loving arms of very personal sympathy are around his children.

This is by no means any praise of contemplatives. It is simply what their vocation requires of them. It is the most ordinary thing in the world. Every year of her life, a cloistered nun should suffer more with others, since love is increasingly dilated by loving, and the capacity to love is always commensurate with the capacity to suffer. Perhaps the only contemplative who can be certain she is in a perilous state is the one who hears with indifferent "detachment" of the need of any soul in the world.

Among the many glories of our generation, there are bound to be some blemishes. And false detachment is one prominent evil of our accelerated tempo of living. We must hurry so fast to go somewhere that we have no time to consider where we are going. Thus we never get anywhere. Always running and never arriving has become a popular modus vivendi, though it certainly achieves nothing as a modus operandi. And in this pursuit, we become unenviably detached both from the small teeming beauties of life all around, and from the pressing little miseries we cannot stop to solace or even to see. We cannot take time for persons when we are accustomed to think in terms of people.

There should be no people in the life of the religious consecrated to God, but only persons. Every religious is called to a Christlike attachment to souls. The contemplative religious is called to a very specialized kind of attachment to them. It is not a case of bettering the lot of The Poor, but of aching in prayer for this one middle-aged father of a large family who is out of a job, for this one widow being defrauded of her small income. There are no groups of Alcoholics Anonymous or Sinners Assorted in the prayer life of a cloistered nun. She is not a club woman in her prayer nor a joiner in her penances. It is not a matter of The Cause, but of multitudinous causes individually espoused.

God's endorsement of the cloistered religious' involvement with the world outside her enclosure walls is shown in many ways. One way is His habit of inspiring those persons outside to send us just what we need at the very moment we need it. It happens so frequently, but we are always newly amazed at it. And it does happen on occasion that we need a rather unusual thing. For instance, a pink evening gown might seem unlikely subject matter for the prayers of petition sent up to heaven by Poor Clare nuns. But this particular autumn, it was what we wanted. It was, in fact, what we needed.

We were planning to produce our play, *Counted as Mine*, for Reverend Mother's feastday; and Mother Vicaress had proven herself a figure of the Gospel householder bringing out of her stores new things and old. We had a rough tilma for Juan Diego, our Lady's little Indian messenger in the Guadalupan apparitions of which this play told the story. The tilma, made of scrubcloths stitched together, was undeniably a masterpiece. We had a jewelled cincture for Juan's wife, Maria Lucia, snatched from the skirt a new postulant had worn into the cloister. We had feathered headdresses for the Indian chorus, supplied by our ducks who had recently given their lives for the cause of the extern Sisters' guests and the costumery of our play. But there was the problem of the star of the production, our Lady.

Even redoubtable Mother Vicaress could not discover any-

thing in her various caches which vaguely resembled the ethe-
real pink floor-length dress required for the Blessed Virgin of
Guadalupe, though she had made postulant Priscilla, who was
cast as our Lady, a glorious blue mantle out of our old grille
curtain, and pasted paper gold stars over it. Then, it came.

We were peeling parsnips that autumn morning, and praying the Franciscan Crown, when Reverend Mother came
from the turn. "I couldn't resist showing you this," she said,
smiling. "Imagine! someone actually sent us an evening
gown!" Mother started to explain that the good lady probably
intended us to cut it up and make dresses for the Infant Jesus of
Prague statue, but she got no further. Several nuns had fallen
upon the dress and were emitting un-nunly squeals of delight.
"Pink!" someone breathed. "And with sequins," another
rhapsodized. "Oh, Mother," we chorused, "it is just exactly
what we need." Now, Reverend Mother can usually face any
situation and have the right word for it. This enthusiastic outpouring, however, quite silenced her.

"May we have it?" pleas were going up. Mother nodded
dumbly, probably from weakness brought on by shock. The
diaphanous pink gown, shooting out sequined light, was swept
off to the infirmary for safekeeping and later discovered to fit
Priscilla perfectly. When the homemade curtain opened on
Counted as Mine, Juan Diego trudged across a darkened
chapter-room floor spread with dry branches and aflutter with
pampas grass from the cloister garden. Then the inner curtain
made of hotel-discard sheets was drawn back, and our Lady
"appeared," the improvised spotlight picking out every starry
sequin on her fabulous pink gown. Priscilla was lovely. Priscilla was an authentic Guadalupan Madonna. "Ah!" we
sighed. Our Lord had done it again.

In her last testament, St. Clare reminds her nuns that they

are to be "a model and a mirror for those who live in the world." Borrowing the thought of St. Paul, she writes to Blessed Agnes of Prague: "I hold you to be a co-worker of God Himself and a support for the frail and failing members of His glorious Body." There was nothing convex about Clare's spirituality or her concept of the significance of her vocation for the world. In her own day, God freely endorsed her ideas, as He endorses them for her daughters today. When she longed for a certain kind of fish and a particular sort of bun for a sick nun, God sent them by a mysterious messenger. When her daughters today long for a pink evening gown, He sends it, too. The smallest need of persons in the world can never be beneath the notice of contemplative religious. And in His turn, God shows that a fish or a bun or a pink sequined dress are not beneath His.

This arrangement makes life very simple. For we know that when God does not send something or arrange for something, it means He does not want us to have it. This means that we no longer want it. In fact, when a religious vocation is reduced to its simplest terms, which are its realest terms, even the smallest details of life have a sturdy realism about them. When our dust storms whirl, and fine brown dust insinuates itself through every crevice, postulant Therese gets out St. Peter's plastic sweater. There his little statue sits on his small bronze throne behind the choir, holding the keys of heaven under his plastic sweater. When the climbing rose decides to climb up the window, we are not allowed to open the out-swinging window panes all summer out of consideration for the rose. There is a very hard-headed practicality in these things. It comes of a determinedly unconvex approach to life in general.

Once we manage to thrust the sword of truth through the

armor of the convex god, we see that all his declared truths are the worst kind of lies, half-truths. He insists that our companions in religion must be held off at a distance in the name of eschewing particular friendships and cliques. He does not want any footnotes added to explain that particular friendship in the evil sense is no friendship at all, and that where holy friendships are, there no cliques are. "Where charity and love are, there God is," we sing in the Church's moving responsory at the *Mandatum* of Holy Thursday. And where God is, the only conceivable clique comprises everyone in the little world of the community and everyone in the larger world outside.

The convex god urges personal sanctification first, last, and betwixt; but he fails to add that personal sanctification is inconceivable without expression in charity. And what he particularly does not wish mentioned is that genuine personal sanctification *is* the most basic kind of outgoing charity. He advocates pushing creatures away in the name of striving for perfection. But he is also shrewd enough to realize that the most availing of all methods for pushing men from Christ is to run to serve them when we have not stored anything of Christ to serve, and so must serve them only ourselves. His armor is unique. He can wear it inside or right side out, as circumstances indicate.

The great need of our time is that the love of Christ be carried everywhere, which is another way of saying that all men everywhere be gathered into the love of Christ. The active religious and the layman will do this by tangible service; the cloistered contemplative, by intangible service. But, either way, it will be service; and service will be more efficacious according as it is more consciously given out of an impelling love. To do this, we may need to comb a few snarls out of our thinking.

A Sister engaged in the active apostolate and seeing the need of a fuller involvement in parochial life will understand that need as a fuller commitment of herself to her vocation, not as an extracurricular activity. Some odd things are being said about a Sister going into the homes of laymen to learn the give-and-take of family life. This presupposes that she has not come from a family of her own, was taught nothing of spiritual psychology and the simple art of family living in her novitiate, and lives now in a malfunctioning community. If she does not understand the give-and-take of family living after years in the convent, it is doubtful that she will get the idea on parish visits. It would be naive to suppose that is the method to unlearn years of convex conventual living.

Better and simpler it is for both active and contemplative religious to probe the mystery of the religious vocation in the silence of prayer. Service will then take its form quite naturally and be a vital service, however diversely rendered. New life and great love will be its blossoming. St. Francis and St. Clare were such vital human beings that they inevitably infused new life into whatever they encountered. Hearts so loving as theirs generated love everywhere, often striking it off the flintiest and most unpromising hearts. It must have been the acutest suffering of their lives to come occasionally upon a human being from whom their intensity of life and their urgency of love could not dynamize a response. Even such persons would surely have seemed to Francis and Clare symbols of Christ entombed, Christ dead, rather than merely the loveless rational animals another might see and reject. Such outgoing love as theirs could never quite be defeated, even when it was rejected.

We talk a great deal and write a very great deal about emotional maturity in religious life. Reduced to fundamentals, we cannot fail to discover that emotional maturity consists not so much in dialogue, adaptation, personality development, or even acceptance of new challenges, as in knowing how to love. It is this single knowledge that is the defeat of the convex god.

September is a month of pathos. It has not yet reached the gorgeous, fevered dying of October. It has passed the ripeness of July and the fullness of August. There is a gentle shagginess about it. And in the heart of its pathos, on September 17, Holy Church celebrates the feast of St. Francis' stigmatization. It was two years before his death. It was well past the crest of his active ministry. He was sick and frail. He had suffered bitter disappointment and betrayal by his own. Who would have blamed Francis if he had then adopted a more convex attitude toward life? Better to retreat into himself and push the hurts of men and the demands of life away. Better to look to himself. But Francis' poor body and seraphic heart were consumed with a great desire. He cried out to God that he might be permitted to bear in his own body, insofar as he could, the pain Christ had endured in His passion and death. And he begged God to let him experience in his heart all the love Christ had felt for men in His redeeming passion. God heard his prayer. He granted it with the stigmata. From that September of 1224 until his death in 1226, Francis bore the five wounds of the Savior visibly on his body. And also from that moment, it was a stigmatized heart that beat in his breast, a heart that held the hearts of all men everywhere.

We shall hope to see those wounds glorified in heaven. But it would be a great pity, even the final tragedy, if the sons or daughters of St. Francis did not come to meet him with stigmatized hearts of their own. This, in fact, is the vocation of all religious, active or contemplative: to have a heart wounded by the love of Christ, a heart for all the world. Some will stretch out their arms to the world in the marketplace. And some will stretch out their arms to the world from the enclosed garden of God. Mankind needs consecrated souls in the midst of it. But mankind also needs that there should be consecrated souls "always in the temple praising and blessing God. Amen." (Luke xxiv,53)